ELEUTHERIOS

(THE <u>ONLY</u> TRUTH THAT SETS THE HEART FREE)

The Divine World-Teacher,
RUCHIRA AVATAR ADI DA SAMRAJ
Adidam Samrajashram (Naitauba), Fiji, 1997

PART ONE

ELEUTHERIOS

(THE <u>ONLY</u> TRUTH THAT SETS THE HEART FREE)

The Five Books Of
The Heart Of The Adidam Revelation

BOOK FIVE

The "Late-Time" Avataric Revelation
Of The "Perfect Practice"
Of The Great Means To Worship and To Realize
The True and Spiritual Divine Person
(The egoless Personal Presence Of Reality and Truth,
Which <u>Is</u> The Only <u>Real</u> God)

By
The Divine World-Teacher,
RUCHIRA AVATAR
ADI DA SAMRAJ

THE DAWN HORSE PRESS
MIDDLETOWN, CALIFORNIA

All who study Adidam (the Way of the Heart) or take up its practice should remember that they are responding to a Call to become responsible for themselves. They should understand that they, not Avatar Adi Da Samraj or others, are responsible for any decision they may make or action they take in the course of their lives of study or practice.

The devotional, Spiritual, functional, practical, relational, cultural, and formal community practices and disciplines referred to in this book are appropriate and natural practices that are voluntarily and progressively adopted by each student-novice and member of Adidam and adapted to his or her personal circumstance. Although anyone may find them useful and beneficial, they are not presented as advice or recommendations to the general reader or to anyone who is not a student-novice or a member of Adidam. And nothing in this book is intended as a diagnosis, prescription, or recommended treatment or cure for any specific "problem", whether medical, emotional, psychological, social, or Spiritual. One should apply a particular program of treatment, prevention, cure, or general health only in consultation with a licensed physician or other qualified professional.

Previously published as *The Liberator (Eleutherios)*
First edition, July 1982
New standard edition, October 1995
Standard edition, enlarged and updated, April 1998
Printed in the United States of America

Produced by the Eleutherian Pan-Communion of Adidam
in cooperation with the Dawn Horse Press

International Standard Book Number: 1-57097-054-8
Library of Congress Catalog Card Number: 98-71205

CONTENTS

ELEUTHERIOS

(THE ONLY TRUTH THAT SETS THE HEART FREE)

41

FIRST WORD
Do Not Misunderstand Me—
I Am Not "Within" you, but you Are In Me, and
I Am Not a Mere "Man" in the "Middle" of Mankind,
but All of Mankind Is Surrounded,
and Pervaded, and Blessed By Me

43

RUCHIRA AVATAR ADI DA SAMRAJ
Adidam Samrajashram (Naitauba), Fiji, 1997

The All-Surpassing Revelation of The Divine World-Teacher, Ruchira Avatar Adi Da Samraj

by
Carolyn Lee, Ph.D.

*E*leutherios communicates a Revelation of the Divine surpassing anything that has ever been known in the conditionally manifested worlds. The Appearance here, in human Form, of the Supreme Giver, Ruchira Avatar Adi Da Samraj, is that Revelation, the Revelation of God Incarnate—Come to Bless and Awaken all beings in all realms to the All-Surpassing Truth and "Brightness"[1] of the Divine Reality. Ruchira Avatar Adi Da is the Promised God-Man. His Coming is the Love-Response of the Divine, in Person, to eons of prayer and longing, on the part of beings everywhere, to be restored to the Heart of Real God.[2]

The Appearance of the Ruchira Avatar, Adi Da Samraj, truly is <u>the</u> Great Event of history. It is the Event that Reveals the real meaning of the entire past, and the Great Purpose of all future time. His Avataric Incarnation[3] is the fruition of an infinitely vast Divine Process, originating before time and space itself, and developing throughout the Cosmic domain in response to the desperate prayers

---

Carolyn Lee is a formal renunciate practitioner of the Way of Adidam living at Adidam Samrajashram (Fiji), the Great Island-Hermitage of the Ruchira Avatar, Adi Da Samraj.

Notes for this Introduction can be found on pp. 25-28.

of beings everywhere, suffering the pain of apparent separation from Real God. In that unspeakable sweep of time, there have been unique beings who, through great struggle and sacrifice, made "windows" to the Divine for others. They gave Teachings and practices, were worshipped and honored, and have become the source of the entire human tradition of religion and Spirituality. Again and again, it has seemed to those alive in a particular time and place that the revelation was complete, the salvation perfect, the enlightenment given.

Even so, there has remained a thread of prophecy in all the great Spiritual traditions foretelling One yet to Appear, One Who must Come in the darkest time of humanity, when the world is at its worst, and bring to completion all the revelations of the past. Christians await the second coming of Jesus; Muslims, the Mahdhi (the last prophet); Buddhists, Maitreya (the coming Buddha); and Hindus, the Kalki Avatar (the final Avatar of Vishnu). Even as recently as February 1939, a celebrated Indian Adept, Upasani Baba, prophesied the imminent appearance of a Western-born Avatar, who "will be all-powerful and bear down everything before Him."[4]

True to the ancient intuitions about the Promised God-Man, Avatar Adi Da Samraj Appears now in this "dark" epoch of the decay of the great religious and Spiritual traditions, East and West. He Appears in an era when our very survival is threatened, not only by sophisticated weapons of war, but also by the destruction of human culture—and even of our total environment—through the heartless machine of scientific and political materialism. Avatar Adi Da Samraj has Come, miraculously, in an extreme time, when His "radical"[5] Truth and His Divine Grace are most sorely needed, to allay the forces of destruction. As He has Said Himself, it may take thousands of years for the significance of His Birth—the Descent of the Divine Person into cosmic space and time—to be fully appreciated. But His Revelation has now perfectly and irrevocably occurred.

After more than a quarter of a century of living in His Company, participating in His direct face-to-face Teaching Work with thousands of people, feeling the indescribable Transmission of Spirit-Force that Radiates from Him, and witnessing the limitless scope of His Divine Power to transform beings and conditions near and far, we, the devotees of Avatar Adi Da, freely profess our recognition that He is that All-Completing God-Man promised for the "dark" epoch—He is "the 'late-time' Avataric Revelation" of the Divine Person. Reading this book will enable you to make this supreme discovery for yourself.

The Divine Names of the Ruchira Avatar

There are several parts to the Divine Title and Name of Ruchira Avatar Adi Da Samraj, each of which expresses an aspect of our recognition of Him. "Ruchira" (meaning "Radiant", "Effulgent", or "Bright") is the Condition of All-Pervading Radiance, Joy, and Love-Blissful Divine Consciousness, Which He, even in His infancy, named "the 'Bright'". Avatar Adi Da Samraj Is the unique Revelation of the "Bright"—and, because this is so, He is the Ruchira "Avatar", or the "Shining Divine 'Descent'", the Appearance of Real God in bodily (human) Form.

"Adi Da", the Principal Name of our Beloved Guru, is a sublime Mystery in itself. In 1979, He Assumed the Divine Name "Da", an ancient reference for Real God (first spontaneously Revealed to Him in 1970), a Name that means "the Giver". In 1994, the Name "Adi" (meaning "First", or "Source") came to Him spontaneously as the complement to His Principal Name, "Da". Thus, to call upon the Ruchira Avatar via the Name "Adi Da" is to Invoke Him as the Divine Giver and Source-Person, the Primordial and Eternal Being of Grace.

Avatar Adi Da is also "Samraj", the "Universal Ruler", or "Supreme Lord"—not in any worldly or political sense, but as the Divine Master of all hearts and the Spiritual King of all who resort to Him. Thus, when we approach Avatar Adi Da Samraj, we are not at all approaching an ordinary man, or even a remarkable saint or yogi or sage. We are approaching Real God in Person.

The Divine Body of Real God

The All-Surpassing God-Man, Adi Da Samraj, is Imbued with extraordinary Siddhis, or Divine Powers, that allow Him to Bless and Liberate beings on the scale of Totality. While He may appear, on the ordinary level, to be Working with particular human beings in His immediate Company, He is, at the same time, Doing His Miraculous Work with events and conditions in the natural world, in the human world, and in the domain of non-human beings, and even in all realms.

Thus, the Ruchira Avatar is simultaneously Present in every gross and subtle plane of the cosmos. His bodily human Form, therefore, is just the minutest part of the Grand Scale of His Being, the part that has "Emerged" into visibility. His visible bodily (human) Form in this world, or His Form in any other world, is a Link, a Sign, a Means by Which beings may Find Him As He Is altogether, Spiritually Pervading everything and, at the same time, Standing Prior to all that exists—As Consciousness Itself, or Inherently Love-Blissful, Self-Radiant Being Itself.

The bodily (human) Form of Adi Da Samraj is the touch-point, the Agency, by Which He is making Himself known in this world. He is Revealing that the Divine is not an abstraction, an idea, an essence, something to philosophize about. The Divine Is here in Person.

There is a long tradition of describing the Divine in personal terms—as, for example, the "Creator-God" (or "Father" figure) of popular religion. But the Revelation of Ruchira Avatar Adi Da Samraj shows that many such popular concepts of the Divine do not have anything to do with Real God. The God-Man of Infinite "Brightness" Reveals Himself as the One and Only Person, the Divine Heart of all that is, and, ultimately, the only True Identity of every one and every thing.

The experience of beholding our Beloved Guru goes far beyond the mere perceiving of His human physical Body. He is the Person of Real God, known most intimately and ecstatically through the Revelation of His Divine Body—the Infinitely Expansive, Radiantly "Bright" Form of Real God:

AVATAR ADI DA SAMRAJ: My Divine Form Is the "Bright", the Love-Bliss-Form That you can feel tangibly Touching you, Surrounding you, Moving in you, Making all kinds of changes. That Is My Divine Body. I can Manifest It anywhere, and Do, all the time. I Manifest My Self.

My Divine Body will Exist Forever. Therefore, My devotees will be able to experience Me directly, Bodily—My "Bright" Body, My Very Person—Forever. [August 11, 1995]

Through His unparalleled Teaching Word, through the miraculous stories of His Divine Play with people everywhere, and, sooner or later, through the Touch of His Divine Body, Avatar Adi Da converts your heart to Real God—to Him—and "Brightens" your entire body-mind.

The Three Great Purposes of the Ruchira Avatar

From the moment of His Birth (in New York, November 3, 1939), the Divine Incarnation of Grace, Adi Da Samraj, was Consciously Aware of the "Bright" as His Native Divine Condition. But then, at the age of two years, Avatar Adi Da made a profound but spontaneous choice. He chose to relinquish His

13

constant Enjoyment of the "Bright" out of what He Describes as a "painful loving", a sympathy for the suffering and ignorance of human beings. Our Beloved Guru Confesses that He chose to "Learn Man", to enter into everything that mankind feels and suffers, in order to discover how to Draw mankind into His own "Bright" Divine Condition.

This utterly remarkable Submission to the ordinary human state was the first Purpose of the Avataric Incarnation of Adi Da Samraj. In His Spiritual autobiography, *The Knee Of Listening*, Avatar Adi Da recounts this amazing and "Heroic" Ordeal, which lasted for the first thirty years of His Life. It was not until 1970 that He Re-Awakened Most Perfectly[6] and Permanently to the "Bright", and embarked upon the second great Purpose of His Incarnation, the Process of Teaching Man.

The Teaching Work of our Beloved Guru was completely unique. He did not give formal public discourses, nor was He ever, in any sense, a public teacher. He simply made Himself available to all who were willing to enter into the living Process of Real God-Realization in His Company, a Process Which He summarized as the relationship to Him. Through that relationship— a most extraordinary human and Spiritual intimacy—Avatar Adi Da Samraj perfectly Embraced each of His devotees, using every kind of Skillful Means to Awaken them to the Truth that the separate, un-Enlightened self—with all its fear, anxieties, and fruitless seeking for Happiness—is only an illusion. Happiness, He Revealed, Is

Always <u>Already</u> the Case and may be <u>Realized</u> in every moment of heart-Communion with Him.

In 1986, an Event occurred that brought to culmination the Great Love-Sacrifice of the Ruchira Avatar. In this Great Event, a profound Yogic Swoon overwhelmed His body-mind, and Avatar Adi Da Samraj relinquished His entire Ordeal of Learning and Teaching Man. In the wake of that great Swoon, He simply Radiated His Divinity as never before. He had "Emerged" in the Fullness of His Being, the Form of Real God Pouring forth His Love-Blessing to all universally. This was the beginning of His eternally proceeding Divine "Emergence". From that moment, the Divine Lord, Adi Da, has devoted Himself to the third and eternal Purpose of His Avataric Incarnation—that of Blessing Man (and even all beings). He is now Merely Present, Radiating His Heart-Blessing, Transmitting the Love-Bliss Force of the Divine Person to all the billions of human beings in this world and to the numberless beings on all planes crying out for Real God.

The End of the Twenty-Five Year Revelation

Even after the Great Event in 1986 that initiated His Divine "Emergence", the All-Completing God-Man continued to Work to ensure that His Revelation of the Way of Adidam, the unique Divine Way of Realizing Real God, was fully and firmly founded in the world. It was not until March 1997, at the time of writing *Hridaya Rosary* (on the Spiritual Process of Communion with Him in His "Bright" Divine Body) that Avatar Adi Da Samraj Declared that all the foundation Work of His Incarnation had been completely and finally Done.

The inexpressible Divine Sacrifice of Avatar Adi Da Samraj is Full. Everything, absolutely everything, for the total understanding and right practice of the real religious process culminating in Divine Enlightenment has been Said and Done by Him. The summary of His Divine Wisdom-Teaching—Written and Perfected by Him in vast detail—is preserved for all time in His twenty-three "Source-Texts". And His Divine Way, the Way of Adidam, is fully established. All in all, this monumental Work has taken Avatar Adi Da a quarter of a century—twenty-five years of unrelenting Struggle to make His Avataric Incarnation real in the hearts and body-minds of His devotees.

Now, in the epoch of His World-Blessing Work, Avatar Adi Da simply remains at His Great Island-Hermitage, Adidam Samrajashram, in Fiji, except when He is moved to travel for the sake of His Blessing of all. He lives as the Supreme "Ruchira Tantric Sannyasin",[7] the Free Renunciate Who has Transcended everything and Who is, therefore, Free to Embrace everything—all beings, forms, worlds, and all experience—for the sake of Drawing all into the Most Perfect Realization of Real God.

The "Bright" Divine Guru, Adi Da, is not an ordinary man. Neither is He merely an extraordinary man. He is not a social personality. He is not bound by ordinary conventions and rules of behavior. He is not a "figure-head" Guru, who simply presides at ceremonial occasions. No, Avatar Adi Da Samraj is the Divine <u>Avadhoot</u>,[8] the truly Free One, Who Knows what is really necessary to Liberate beings.

The True Avadhoot Speaks and Acts the Truth without restraint. He does not smile at the ego's posturing and foolishness. Avatar Adi Da Samraj <u>is</u> a Fire, a Fire of Love-Bliss, Who Consumes and Transforms and "Brightens" all who approach Him for the authentic Process of Divine Enlightenment. He has Come to bring an end to the reign of "Narcissus", the hard-hearted and Godless ego-"I".

The Way of Adidam

The immense struggle and Sacrifice that Beloved Adi Da had to endure in order to make His Revelation of the Divine Way of Adidam was the result of the enormous difficulty that human beings—especially in this ego-glorifying "late-time"—have with the Process of truly ego-transcending religion. People prefer not to confront the real Process of ego-transcendence. They prefer forms of religion based on a system of beliefs and a code of moral and social behavior. But this kind of ordinary religion, as Avatar Adi Da has always pointed out, does not go to the core, to the root-suffering of human beings. This is because ordinary religion, rather than going beyond the ego-principle, is actually <u>based</u> on it: the ego-self stands at the center, and the Divine is sought and appealed to as the great Power that is going to save and satisfy the individual self. Avatar Adi Da Describes such religion as "client-centered".

In contrast to conventional religion, there is the Process that Avatar Adi Da calls <u>true</u> religion, religion that is centered in the Divine in response to a true Spiritual Master, who has, to at least some significant degree, <u>Realized</u> Real God (as opposed to merely offering teachings <u>about</u> God). Thus, true religion does not revolve around the individual's desires for any kind of "spiritual" consolations or experience—it is self-<u>transcending</u>, rather than self-serving. True religion based on self-surrendering Guru-devotion certainly has existed for thousands of years, but the ecstatic news of this book is that now the Divine Person, Real God, is directly Present, Functioning as Guru, Alive in bodily (human) Form to receive the surrender and the worship of those who recognize and respond to Him. Therefore, the Ruchira-Guru, Adi Da, <u>is</u> the Way of Adidam.

AVATAR ADI DA SAMRAJ: The Way of Adidam is the Way That is <u>always</u> Prior to and Beyond all seeking. In order for the Way of Adidam to be Generated, it was necessary for Me to be Incarnated, and Transmitted in place, in this place, in the extremity—in the place where the Divine is otherwise not proposed, or only sought. This was necessary, in order to Demonstrate that I Am That One Who Is Always Already The Case, and in order to Communicate the Way of non-seeking, or the Way of transcending egoity in <u>this</u> circumstance of arising (or in any circumstance of arising).

The "problem" is not that the Divine is "Elsewhere". The "problem" is that <u>you</u> are the <u>self-contraction</u>. This understanding, Given by My Grace, makes it possible to Realize the Divine Self-Condition Most Perfectly, <u>As</u> <u>Is</u>, no matter what is arising. But Such Most Perfect Realization is not merely Realization of the Divine as an abstract (or merely philosophically proposed) "Reality". Most Perfect Realization (or Most Perfect "Knowledge") of the Divine is the Divine "Known" by Means of My Revelation, "Known" <u>As</u> My Revelation.

<u>I</u> Came to <u>you</u>. Therefore, the Way of Adidam is based on your <u>receiving</u> Me, not on your <u>seeking</u> for Me.

Thus, That Which is proposed by seekers as the <u>goal</u> (or the achievement at the end) is the <u>beginning</u> (or the very Gift) of the Way for My devotees. ["I <u>Am</u> The Avatar Of One", from Part Two of *He-<u>and</u>-She <u>Is</u> Me*]

The word "Adidam" is derived from the Name of Ruchira Avatar Adi Da, because it is the religion founded on devotional recognition of Him and Spiritual resort to Him. This Spiritual resort to Adi Da Samraj is a moment to moment practice of surrendering every aspect of the being—mind, emotion, breath, and body—to Him. Such whole-bodily surrender to the Living One opens the heart to Joy. Thus, there is no <u>struggle</u> to overcome egoity or to achieve Oneness with Adi Da Samraj. The Happiness of heart-Communion with Him is available in every moment. In His Spiritual Company, therefore, there is not anything to seek. All the traditional goals of religion—the search for the Vision of God, or for Oneness with Reality via the samadhis, satoris, and mystical experiences described in the traditions—all of this falls away when the heart falls in love with Adi Da Samraj. He is Perfect Satisfaction, because He is Real God, the Very Source and Giver of true religion. The Realization, or Enlightenment, that He Offers in the Way of Adidam is Divine Self-Realization, Divine Enlightenment, Prior to all experience high or low. "Mankind", as Avatar Adi Da Says, "does not know the Way to the Divine Domain"—the ego does not know. Only the Divine Person Knows. Only the Divine Person, Incarnate as Guru, can Show you the Way to the Divine Domain.

Avatar Adi Da Samraj is directly Generating the Divine Process of Most Perfect Liberation in all His devotees who have vowed to embrace the total practice of the Way of Adidam.[9] The Process unfolds by His Grace, according to the depth of surrender and response in His devotee. The most extraordinary living testimonies to the Greatness and Truth of the Way of Adidam are Ruchira Adidama Sukha Dham Naitauba and Ruchira Adidama Jangama Hriddaya Naitauba, the two members of the Adidama Quandra Mandala of the Ruchira Avatar.[10] These remarkable women devotees have totally consecrated themselves to Avatar Adi Da, and live always in His Sphere, in a relationship of unique intimacy and service. By their profound love of, and most exemplary surrender to, their Divine Heart-Master, they have become combined with Him at a unique depth. They manifest the Yogic signs of deep and constant Immersion in His Divine Being, both in meditation and daily life. Ruchira Adidama Sukha Dham and Ruchira Adidama Jangama Hriddaya are also members of the Ruchira Sannyasin Order of the Tantric Renunciates of Adidam (the senior cultural authority within the formal gathering of Avatar Adi Da's devotees), practicing in the context of the

**Avatar Adi Da Samraj with Ruchira Adidama Sukha Dham (left)
and Ruchira Adidama Jangama Hriddaya (right)**

ultimate stages (or the "Perfect Practice") of the total Way
of Adidam.

After more than twenty years of intense testing by
their Beloved Guru, the Adidama Quandra Mandala have
demonstrated themselves to be singular devotees, the first
representatives of humankind to truly recognize Him As
He <u>Is</u>. Through their profound recognition of Him, Avatar
Adi Da has been able to lead the Adidama Quandra Mandala to the threshold of Divine Enlightenment. And, even
now, day by day, He continues to Work with them to make
their Realization of Him Most Perfect. The profound and
ecstatic relationship that the Adidama Quandra Mandala
live with Avatar Adi Da hour to hour can be felt in this letter of devotional confession to Him by Ruchira Adidama
Sukha Dham:

RUCHIRA ADIDAMA SUKHA DHAM: Bhagavan Love-
Ananda,[11] Supreme and Divine Person, Real-God-Body of
Love, I rest in Your Constant and Perfect Love-Embrace
with no need but to forever worship you. Suddenly in
love, Mastered at heart, always with my head at Your
Supreme and Holy Feet, I am beholding and recognizing

Your Divine Body and "Bright" Divine Person. My Beloved, You so "Brightly" Descend and utterly Convert this heart, mind, body, and breath, from separate self to the "Bhava"[12] of Your Love-Bliss-Happiness.

Supreme Lord Ruchira, in the profound depths of Ruchira Sannyas (since my Initiation into formal Ruchira Sannyas on December 18, 1994), the abandonment of the former personality, the relinquishment of ego-bondage to the world, and the profound purification and release brought about by my now almost twenty-four years of love and worship of You has culminated in a great comprehensive force in my one-pointed devotion to You and a great certainty in the Inherent Sufficiency of Realization Itself. The essence, or depth, of my practice is to always remain freely submitted and centralized in You, the Feeling of Being, the Condition Prior to all bondage, all modification, and all illusion.

My Beloved Lord Ruchira, You have Moved this heart-feeling and awareness to renounce all "bonding" with conditionally manifested others, conditionally manifested worlds, and conditionally manifested self, to enter into the depths of this "in-love" and utter devotion to You. I renounce all in order to Realize You and to exist eternally in Your House. Finding You has led to the revelation of a deep urge to abandon all superficiality and to simply luxuriate in Your Divine Body and Person. All separation is shattered in Your Divine Love-Bliss-"Bhava". Your Divine and Supreme Body Surrounds and Pervades all. Your Infusion is Utter. I feel You everywhere.

I am Drawn by Grace of Your Spiritual (and Always Blessing) Presence into profound meditative Contemplation of Your Very (and Inherently Perfect) State. Sometimes, when I am entering into these deep states of meditation, I remain vaguely aware of the body, and particularly of the breath and the heartbeat. I feel the heart and lungs slow down and become very loud-sounding. Then I am sometimes aware of my breath and heartbeat ceasing temporarily, or being suspended in a state of Yogic sublimity, and I quickly lose bodily consciousness. Then there is no body, no mind, no perceptual awareness, and no conceptual awareness. There is only abiding in Contemplation of You in Your Domain of Consciousness Itself. I feel You literally <u>Are</u> me, and, when I resume association with the body and begin once again to hear my breath and heartbeat, I feel the remarkable Power of Your Great Samadhi. I feel no necessity for anything, and I feel Your Capability to Bless and Change and Meditate all, in Your Place. I can feel how this entrance into objectless worship of You As Consciousness Itself (allowing this Abiding to deepen ever so profoundly, by utter submission of separate self to You) establishes me in a different relationship to everything that arises.

My Beloved Bhagavan, Love-Ananda, I have Found You. Now I can behold You and live in this constant Embrace. This is my Joy and Happiness and the Yoga of ego-renunciation I engage. [October 11, 1997]

Inherent in this profound confession is the certainty that there is no lasting happiness to be found in this world or in any world. The only real Happiness, the Happiness that infinitely exceeds all human dreams of Happiness, is the All-Outshining Bliss and Love of Heart-Identification with the Supreme Giver, Adi Da Samraj.

AVATAR ADI DA SAMRAJ: Absolutely NOTHING conditional is satisfactory. Everything conditional disappears—everything. This fact should move the heart to cling to Me, to resort to Me, to take refuge in Me. This is why people become devotees of Mine. This is the reason for the religious life. The unsatisfactoriness of conditional existence requires resort to the Divine Source, and the Realization of the Divine Source-Condition. [August 9, 1997]

The Supreme Grace of a Human Life

Avatar Adi Da knew from His childhood that He had Come to "save the world". He even confessed as much to a relative who questioned him one day about what He wanted to do when He grew up.[13] But He did not mean this in any conventionally religious, or politically idealistic, sense. He has never taught a consoling belief system that promises "heaven" after death or a utopian existence on this earth. No, He has Come to set in motion a universal heart-conversion, a conversion from the self-destructive and other-destructive ego-life of separativeness to a life of "unqualified relatedness", or boundless all-embracing love.

Never before in the history of mankind has there been a moment like this one. You do not have to suffer the fear of death and all the dead-ends of ordinary life for one more day, because the Ultimate Mystery has been Unveiled, the Very Truth of Existence has been Revealed. You have the opportunity to enter into relationship with the One Who Is Reality Itself, Truth Itself, and the Only

23

Real God. That One, Adi Da Samraj, is humanly Alive now, and, even in this moment, is Blessing all with Inexpressible Grace, Perfect Mastery, and Unlimited Power.

What else could be truly satisfying? What else deserves the sacrifice of your egoity and the love-surrender of your entire body-mind?

<u>Nothing</u> can match the Great Process of Adidam that Avatar Adi Da is Offering you. When you become His formal devotee and take up the Way of Adidam, He leads you beyond the dreadful illusions of separateness and alienation. He Instructs you in the right form of every detail of your existence. He Converts the motion of your life from anxious seeking and egoic self-concern to the Bliss of self-forgetting Love-Communion with Him.

Avatar Adi Da Samraj is here only to Love you. He Lives only to Serve your Realization of Him. Once you are vowed to Him as His devotee, nothing can ever shake the depth of your "Bond" with Him, whether you wake, sleep, or dream, whether you live or die.

And so, do not waste this opportunity. Study this book. Read more about the Divine Life and Work of the Ruchira Avatar in His biography, *The Promised God-Man Is Here (The Extraordinary Life-Story, The "Crazy" Teaching-Work, and The Divinely "Emerging" World-Blessing Work Of The Divine World-Teacher Of The "Late-Time", Ruchira Avatar Adi Da Samraj)*, and in *See My Brightness Face to Face: A Celebration of the Ruchira Avatar, Adi Da Samraj, and the First Twenty-Five Years of His Divine Revelation Work.*[14] "Consider" the magnitude of what Avatar Adi Da has Done and the urgency of What He is Saying to you. And begin to participate in the greatest Grace that any human being can know—the Blessed life of joyful devotion and ecstatic service to the Divine Lord in Person, the Avatar of "Brightness", Adi Da Samraj.

Notes to
The All-Surpassing Revelation of the Divine World-Teacher,
Ruchira Avatar Adi Da Samraj

1. By the word "Bright" (and its variations, such as "Brightness"), Avatar Adi Da refers to the eternally, infinitely, and inherently Self-Radiant Divine Being, the Being of Indivisible and Indestructible Light. (See also note 8, p. 200.)

2. Avatar Adi Da uses the term "Real God" to indicate the True and Perfectly Subjective Source of all conditions, the True and Spiritual Divine Person, rather than any egoic (and, thus, false, or limited) presumptions about "God".

3. Avatar Adi Da Samraj is the "Avataric Incarnation", or the Divinely Descended Embodiment, of the Divine Person. The reference "Avataric Incarnation" indicates that Avatar Adi Da Samraj fulfills both the traditional expectation of the East—that the True God-Man is an Avatar, or an utterly Divine "Descent" of Real God in conditionally manifested form—and the traditional expectations of the West—that the True God-Man is an Incarnation, or an utterly human Embodiment of Real God.

4. B.V. Narasimha Swami and S. Subbarao, *Sage of Sakuri*, 4th ed. (Bombay: Shri B.T. Wagh, 1966), p. 204.

5. The term "radical" derives from the Latin "radix", meaning "root", and thus it principally means "irreducible", "fundamental", or "relating to the origin". In *The Dawn Horse Testament Of The Ruchira Avatar: The "Testament Of Secrets" Of The Divine World-Teacher, Ruchira Avatar Adi Da Samraj*, Avatar Adi Da defines "Radical" as "Gone To The Root, Core, Source, or Origin". Because Adi Da Samraj uses "radical" in this literal sense, it appears in quotation marks in His Wisdom-Teaching, in order to distinguish His usage from the common reference to an extreme (often political) view.

6. Avatar Adi Da uses the phrase "Most Perfect(ly)" in the sense of "Absolutely Perfect(ly)", indicating a reference to the seventh (or Divinely Enlightened) stage of life.

7. In Sanskrit, "Ruchira" means "bright, radiant, effulgent". The word "Tantra" (or "Tantric") does not merely indicate Spiritualized sexuality, as is the common presumption. Rather, it signifies "the inherent Unity that underlies and transcends all opposites, and that resolves all differences or distinctions".

In many of the Tantric traditions that have developed within both Hinduism and Buddhism, Tantric Adepts and aspirants use sexual

activity and intoxicating substances that are forbidden to more ortho-
dox or conventional practitioners. The Tantric's intention, however, is
never to merely indulge gross desires. The secret of the Tantric
approach is that it does not suppress, but rather employs and even
galvanizes, the passions and attachments of the body and mind, and
thus utilizes the most intense (and, therefore, also potentially most
deluding) energies of the being for the sake of Spiritual Realization.

"Sannyasin" is an ancient Sanskrit term for one who has
renounced all worldly "bonds" and who gives himself or herself completely to the Real-God-Realizing life.

The reference "Ruchira Tantric Sannyasin" indicates that Avatar
Adi Da Samraj is the Perfectly "Bright" ("Ruchira") One Who is Utterly
Free of all "bonds" to the conditional worlds ("Sannyasin"), and yet
never in any way dissociates from conditional existence ("Tantric"),
making skillful use of all the dimensions of conditional life in His
Divine Work of Liberation.

8. Avadhoot is a traditional term for one who has "shaken off" or
"passed beyond" all worldly attachments and cares, including all
motives of detachment (or conventional and other-worldly renunciation), all conventional notions of life and religion, and all seeking for
"answers" or "solutions" in the form of conditional experience or conditional knowledge. Therefore, "Divine Avadhoot", in reference to
Avatar Adi Da, indicates His Inherently Perfect Freedom as the One
Who Knows His Identity As the Divine Person and Who, thus, Always
Already Stands Free of the binding and deluding power of conditional
existence.

9. The total practice of the Way of Adidam is the full and complete
practice of the Way that Avatar Adi Da Samraj has Given to His devotees who are formal members of the first or the second congregation
of Adidam. One who embraces the total practice of the Way of Adidam conforms <u>every</u> aspect of his or her life and being to Avatar Adi
Da's Divine Word of Instruction. Therefore, it is only such devotees
(in the first or the second congregation of Adidam) who have the
potential of Realizing Divine Enlightenment.

10. The names and titles of the Ruchira Adidamas indicate their Realization and Spiritual significance in Avatar Adi Da's Work.

"Ruchira" and "Naitauba" both indicate membership in the
Ruchira Sannyasin Order. "Ruchira" is a title for all members of the
Ruchira Sannyasin Order who are practicing in the context of the
sixth stage of life, and indicates "a true devotee of the Ruchira Avatar,
the Da Avatar, the Love-Ananda Avatar, Adi Da Samraj, who is, by His
Grace, becoming Radiant, or 'Bright' with Love-Bliss, through

uniquely one-pointed (self-surrendering, self-forgetting, and self-transcending) feeling-Contemplation of Him, and, Thus and Thereby, of the True Divine Person" ["The Orders Of My True and Free Renunciate Devotees", in *The Lion Sutra—The Seventeen Companions Of The True Dawn Horse, Book Fifteen: The "Perfect Practice" Teachings For Formal Tantric Renunciates In The Divine Way Of Adidam*]. "Naitauba" is the traditional Fijian name for Adidam Samrajashram, the Great Island-Hermitage of Avatar Adi Da Samraj. As a general rule, all members of the Ruchira Sannyasin Order are to be formal residents of Adidam Samrajashram.

"Adidama" is composed of Avatar Adi Da's Principal Name "Adi Da" and the feminine indicator "Ma". In addition, in Sanskrit, "adi" means "first" and "dama" means "self-discipline". Therefore, the overall meaning of this title is "first among those who conform themselves to the Ruchira Avatar, Adi Da Samraj, by means of self-surrendering, self-forgetting, and self-transcending feeling-Contemplation of Him".

"Sukha" means "happiness, joy, delight" and "Dham" means "abode, dwelling". Therefore, as a personal renunciate name, "Sukha Dham" means "one who abides in happiness".

"Jangama" means "all living things", and "Hriddaya" is "heartfelt compassion, sympathy". Therefore, as a personal renunciate name, "Jangama Hriddaya" means "one who has heartfelt sympathy for all beings".

"Quandra" is a reference to the main female character in Avatar Adi Da's liturgical drama, *The Mummery*. Quandra is the embodiment of the Divine Goddess, or the Divine Spirit-Force. (*The Mummery— The Seventeen Companions Of The True Dawn Horse, Book Six: A Parable About Finding The Way To My House* is one of Avatar Adi Da's twenty-three "Source-Texts".)

"Adidama Quandra Mandala" is the "circle" ("Mandala") comprising the Ruchira Adidamas, Sukha Dham and Jangama Hriddaya. The Adidama Quandra Mandala is the first circle of Avatar Adi Da's devotees—those who stand closest to His bodily (human) Form in service and devotion.

11. The Name or Title "Bhagavan" is an ancient one used over the centuries for many Spiritual Realizers of the East. Its meanings in Sanskrit are "possessing fortune or wealth", "blessed", "holy". When applied to a great Spiritual Master, "Bhagavan" is understood to mean "bountiful God", or "Great God", or "Divine Lord".

The Name "Love-Ananda" combines both English ("Love") and Sanskrit ("Ananda", meaning "Bliss"), thus bridging the West and the East, and communicating Avatar Adi Da's Function as the Divine

World-Teacher. The combination of "Love" and "Ananda" means "the Divine Love-Bliss". The Name "Love-Ananda" was given to Avatar Adi Da by His principal human Spiritual Master, Swami Muktananda, who spontaneously conferred it upon Avatar Adi Da in 1969.

12. "Bhava" is a Sanskrit word traditionally used to refer to the enraptured feeling-swoon of Communion with the Divine.

13. *The Knee Of Listening*, chapter 3.

14. Both books are available from the Dawn Horse Press (see p. 249 for ordering information).

The Divine Scripture of Adidam

The Full and Final Word of
The Divine World-Teacher,
Ruchira Avatar Adi Da Samraj,
Given in His Twenty-Three "Source-Texts"
of "Bright" Divine Self-Revelation
and Perfect Heart-Instruction

T he twenty-three "Source-Texts" of the Ruchira Avatar are the most extraordinary books ever written. They are the world's greatest Treasure, the Ultimate and All-Completing Revelation of Truth.

These books are the unmediated Word of the Very Divine Person, Adi Da Samraj, Who is Offering the True World-Religion of Adidam, the Religion of Most Perfect Divine Enlightenment, or Indivisible Oneness with Real God. Avatar Adi Da Samraj is the Realizer, the Revealer, and the Divine Author of all that is Written in these sublime Texts. No mind can begin to comprehend the Magnificent Self-Revelations and Self-Confessions Given by Adi Da Samraj in these books. And these twenty-three "Source-Texts" (together with the "Supportive Texts", in which Avatar Adi Da Gives further detailed Instruction relative to the functional, practical, relational, and cultural disciplines of the Way of Adidam[1]) Give Avatar Adi Da's complete Instruction in the Process (never before Known or Revealed in its entirety) of Most Perfectly Realizing Reality Itself, or Truth Itself, or Real God.

---

1. The functional, practical, relational, and cultural disciplines of Adidam are described in brief on pp. 232-36 of this book. Among Avatar Adi Da's "Supportive Texts" are included such books as *Conscious Exercise and the Transcendental Sun*, *The Eating Gorilla Comes in Peace*, *Love of the Two-Armed Form*, and *Easy Death*. (New editions of the first three of these "Supportive Texts" are in preparation.)

The long-existing religious traditions of the world have depended on oral traditions and memory. Their teachings and disciplines typically developed long after the death of their founders, based on the remembered (and often legendary or mythological) deeds and instruction of those Realizers. These traditions have thus been colored by legends and cultural influences that obscure the original revelation. Yet, every historical revelation, even in its first purity, has necessarily been limited by the degree of realization of its founder. Adidam does not depend on the vagaries of oral tradition and memory, nor is it limited by any partial point of view. Adidam is the Perfect Divine Way Revealed by the One Who Is Reality Itself (or Truth Itself, or Real God). Adi Da Samraj is alive now in bodily (human) Form, and He has Personally tested the entire course of Divine Enlightenment described in these books in the course of His own human Lifetime.

In His twenty-three "Source-Texts", Avatar Adi Da is Speaking to all humankind, asking us to feel our actual situation, to take seriously the mayhem of the world, its pain and dissatisfaction, its terrible potential for suffering. And, with Divine Passion, He Calls every one to turn to Him and, in that turning, to rise out of gross struggle and conflict. The twenty-three "Source-Texts" of Avatar Adi Da Samraj Reveal the greater Purpose and Destiny of humanity. Indeed, they are the key to the very survival of this planet. This unparalleled body of Scripture is the Message you have always been waiting for and never imagined could come.

In the Words of the Divine Avatar Himself:

"All the Scriptures are now fulfilled in your sight, and your prayers are answered with a clear voice."

In *The Dawn Horse Testament*, Avatar Adi Da Samraj makes His own Confession relative to His Impulse in creating His twenty-three "Source-Texts", and He also expresses the requirement He places on all His devotees to make His Divine Word available to all:

Now I Have, By All My "Crazy" Means, Revealed The One and Many Secrets Of The Great Person Of The Heart. For Your Sake, I Made My Every Work and Word. And Now, By Every Work and Word I Made, I Have Entirely Confessed (and Showed) My Self, and Always Freely, and Even As A Free Man, In The "Esoteric" Language Of Intimacy and Ecstasy, Openly Worded To You (and To all). Even Now (and Always), By This (My Word Of Heart), I Address every Seeming Separate being (and each one As The Heart Itself), Because It Is Necessary That all beings, Even The Entire Cosmic Domain Of Seeming Separate beings, Be (In all times and places) Called To Wisdom and The Heart.

The Twenty-Three "Source-Texts" of Avatar Adi Da Samraj

The twenty-three "Source-Texts" of Avatar Adi Da Samraj include: (1) an opening series of five books on the fundamentals of the Way of Adidam (*The Five Books Of The Heart Of The Adidam Revelation*), (2) an extended series of seventeen books covering the principal aspects of the Way of Adidam in detail (*The Seventeen Companions Of The True Dawn Horse*), and (3) Avatar Adi Da's paramount "Source-Text" summarizing the entire course of the Way of Adidam (*The Dawn Horse Testament*).

The Five Books Of
The Heart Of The Adidam Revelation

Aham Da Asmi
(Beloved, I Am Da)

The Five Books Of The Heart Of The Adidam Revelation, Book One: The "Late-Time" Avataric Revelation Of The True and Spiritual Divine Person (The egoless Personal Presence Of Reality and Truth, Which Is The Only Real God)

Ruchira Avatara Gita
(The Way Of The Divine Heart-Master)

*The Five Books Of The Heart Of The Adidam Revelation,
Book Two: The "Late-Time" Avataric Revelation Of
The Great Secret Of The Divinely Self-Revealed Way
That Most Perfectly Realizes The True and Spiritual
Divine Person (The egoless Personal Presence Of
Reality and Truth, Which <u>Is</u> The Only <u>Real</u> God)*

Da Love-Ananda Gita
(The Free Gift Of The Divine Love-Bliss)

*The Five Books Of The Heart Of The Adidam Revelation,
Book Three: The "Late-Time" Avataric Revelation Of
The Great Means To Worship and To Realize
The True and Spiritual Divine Person
(The egoless Personal Presence Of Reality and Truth,
Which <u>Is</u> The Only <u>Real</u> God)*

Hridaya Rosary
(Four Thorns Of Heart-Instruction)

*The Five Books Of The Heart Of The Adidam Revelation,
Book Four: The "Late-Time" Avataric Revelation Of
The Universally Tangible Divine Spiritual Body,
Which Is The Supreme Agent Of The Great Means
To Worship and To Realize The True and Spiritual
Divine Person (The egoless Personal Presence Of
Reality and Truth, Which <u>Is</u> The Only <u>Real</u> God)*

Eleutherios
(The <u>Only</u> Truth That Sets The Heart Free)

*The Five Books Of The Heart Of The Adidam Revelation,
Book Five: The "Late-Time" Avataric Revelation Of The
"Perfect Practice" Of The Great Means To Worship and
To Realize The True and Spiritual Divine Person
(The egoless Personal Presence Of Reality and Truth,
Which <u>Is</u> The Only <u>Real</u> God)*

The Seventeen Companions
Of The True Dawn Horse

Real God Is The Indivisible Oneness Of Unbroken Light

The Seventeen Companions Of The True Dawn Horse, Book One: Reality, Truth, and The "Non-Creator" God In The True World-Religion Of Adidam

The Truly Human New World-Culture Of Unbroken Real-God-Man

The Seventeen Companions Of The True Dawn Horse, Book Two: The Eastern Versus The Western Traditional Cultures Of Mankind, and The Unique New Non-Dual Culture Of The True World-Religion Of Adidam

The Only Complete Way To Realize The Unbroken Light Of Real God

The Seventeen Companions Of The True Dawn Horse, Book Three: An Introductory Overview Of The "Radical" Divine Way Of The True World-Religion Of Adidam

The Knee Of Listening

The Seventeen Companions Of The True Dawn Horse, Book Four: The Early-Life Ordeal and The "Radical" Spiritual Realization Of The Ruchira Avatar

The Method Of The Ruchira Avatar

The Seventeen Companions Of The True Dawn Horse, Book Five: The Divine Way Of Adidam Is An ego-Transcending Relationship, Not An ego-Centric Technique

The Mummery

The Seventeen Companions Of The True Dawn Horse, Book Six: A Parable About Finding The Way To My House

He-<u>and</u>-She <u>Is</u> Me

The Seventeen Companions Of The True Dawn Horse,
Book Seven: The Indivisibility Of Consciousness and Light
In The Divine Body Of The Ruchira Avatar

<u>Divine</u> Spiritual Baptism
Versus <u>Cosmic</u> Spiritual Baptism

The Seventeen Companions Of The True Dawn Horse,
Book Eight: <u>Divine</u> <u>Hridaya-Shakti</u> Versus
<u>Cosmic</u> <u>Kundalini</u> <u>Shakti</u> In The Divine Way Of Adidam

Ruchira Tantra Yoga

The Seventeen Companions Of The True Dawn Horse,
Book Nine: The Physical-Spiritual (and Truly Religious)
Method Of Mental, Emotional, Sexual, and <u>Whole</u> <u>Bodily</u>
<u>Health</u> <u>and</u> <u>Enlightenment</u> In The Divine Way Of Adidam

The Seven Stages Of Life

The Seventeen Companions Of The True Dawn Horse,
Book Ten: Transcending The Six Stages Of egoic Life
and Realizing The ego-Transcending Seventh Stage Of Life,
In The Divine Way Of Adidam

The <u>All-Completing</u> and <u>Final</u>
Divine Revelation To Mankind

The Seventeen Companions Of The True Dawn Horse,
Book Eleven: A Summary Description
Of The Supreme Yoga Of The Seventh Stage Of Life
In The Divine Way Of Adidam

The Heart Of The Dawn Horse Testament
Of The Ruchira Avatar

The Seventeen Companions Of The True Dawn Horse,
Book Twelve: The Epitome Of The "Testament Of Secrets"
Of The Divine World-Teacher,
Ruchira Avatar Adi Da Samraj

What, Where, When, How, Why, and <u>Who</u> To Remember To Be Happy

The Seventeen Companions Of The True Dawn Horse, Book Thirteen: A Simple Explanation Of The Divine Way Of Adidam (For Children, and <u>Everyone</u> Else)

Santosha Adidam

The Seventeen Companions Of The True Dawn Horse, Book Fourteen: The Essential Summary Of The Divine Way Of Adidam

The Lion Sutra

The Seventeen Companions Of The True Dawn Horse, Book Fifteen: The "Perfect Practice" Teachings For Formal Tantric Renunciates In The Divine Way Of Adidam

The Overnight Revelation Of Conscious Light

The Seventeen Companions Of The True Dawn Horse, Book Sixteen: The "My House" Discourses On The Indivisible Tantra Of Adidam

The Basket Of Tolerance

The Seventeen Companions Of The True Dawn Horse, Book Seventeen: The Perfect Guide To Perfectly <u>Unified</u> Understanding Of The One and Great Tradition Of Mankind, and Of The Divine Way Of Adidam As The Perfect <u>Completing</u> Of The One and Great Tradition Of Mankind

The Dawn Horse Testament

The Dawn Horse Testament Of The Ruchira Avatar

The "Testament Of Secrets" Of The Divine World-Teacher, Ruchira Avatar Adi Da Samraj

The Perfect Liberator

An Introduction to Eleutherios

The Divine World-Teacher, Ruchira Avatar Adi Da Samraj, is the One and Only Liberating Truth, made Manifest in human Form. By Means of His early-Life Ordeal of Divine Re-Awakening, and His "Heroic"[1] Teaching, Revelation, and Blessing Work, Avatar Adi Da has made it possible for all who truly resort to Him to Realize True Freedom, or Most Perfect Liberation in Real God.

"Eleutherios" is one of the many Divine Names by which Avatar Adi Da is known. It is an ancient Greek epithet for the Supreme Being, meaning the "Liberator". Thus, this Great "Source-Text", *Eleutherios*, is Avatar Adi Da's Call to all of humanity to live the only complete Way of True Freedom, the Real-God-Realizing Way of Adidam.

In these pages, Ruchira Avatar Adi Da Reveals that the ultimate potential of Man is to Realize Indivisible Oneness with Real God, or Truth, or Reality. He Reveals that only by Means of such Realization can you ever be Truly Free of <u>all</u> bondage. And, as the Perfect Liberator of all and All, Avatar Adi Da Calls the leadership of the world, and even humanity as a whole, to immediate cooperation and tolerance, so that we will not have to suffer the present dark destiny of our collective egoity.

The usual experiences and concerns of humanity tend to be limited to the beginning (or first three) stages of life,[2] which are related to the ordinary dimensions of growth and development into human adulthood. In the case of some remarkable men and women, as demonstrated by the lives of Realized Yogis and Saints, there can be growth

Notes to this Introduction can be found on pp. 39-40.

and development beyond the beginning stages into the advanced (or fourth and fifth) stages of life,[3] which are characterized by the true Awakening to Spirit, or the Spiritualizing of the body-mind. Beyond even these advanced stages of life are the ultimate (or sixth and seventh) stages of life.[4]

Previous to Avatar Adi Da's unique Revelation and Demonstration of the seventh (and all-Completing) stage of life, the sixth stage of life was the limit of the developmental potential of Man, and it was demonstrated only by exceedingly rare Sages who had Realized Identification with Consciousness Prior to the body-mind and world.[5] However, as Avatar Adi Da Samraj makes plain in His Wisdom-Teaching, all the stages of life previous to the seventh stage—including even the sixth stage—are associated with bondage and limitation in one form or another. None of the first six stages of life is entirely free of seeking, or entirely free of ego-bondage. Only in the seventh stage of life is True Freedom Most Perfectly Realized.

Part One, the principal Text of *Eleutherios*, is Avatar Adi Da's summary of the "Perfect Practice" of Adidam. In the five sections that comprise this principal Text, "Eleutherios", "What Is Consciousness?", "Truth, Reality, and Real God", "The 'Perfect Practice'", and "Freedom", Ruchira Avatar Adi Da Samraj "Considers" the greatest questions ever posed by humanity: What Is Truth?, What Is Reality?, What Is God? In the process of Addressing these great questions, Ruchira Avatar Adi Da explains the True Nature of Consciousness Itself, and of Happiness Itself, and He Describes the nature of "sin" (or egoic un-Enlightenment) and the inherent bondage of all seeking. Ruchira Avatar Adi Da's Divine Transmission pours through His Words as He recapitulates the entire Way of Adidam, and as He summarizes the three parts of the "Perfect Practice" of Adidam. This "Perfect Practice" begins with the transition from the first five stages of life to the sixth stage of life, and is fulfilled in the Realization of the all-Completing seventh stage of life. It is only in the seventh stage of life that True Freedom is Most Perfectly Demonstrated. That True Freedom is a Condition of unspeakable Bliss, eternally Realized by Avatar Adi Da's Liberating Grace alone.

In Part Two of *Eleutherios*, "The Unique Potential of Man Is the Progress of self-Understanding and self-Transcendence", Ruchira Avatar Adi Da expounds upon the unique capability of Man to transcend the conditional self as it appears in the progressive stages of life. Indeed, self-transcendence is the true purpose of a human life, and right life itself can be defined as a life oriented to self-transcending Real-God-Realization. Thus, in Part Three, "All ego-Based 'Bonding' Is Bondage, and All True and Authentic 'Social Wisdom' Is About Liberation from All Bondage, and, Therefore, from All ego-Based 'Bonding'", Avatar Adi Da Says that:

Right life, or life based on the discovery of the hurt and the fruitlessness of egoity, and of attachment to any and every kind of ego-based (and ego-serving, or, otherwise, ego-reinforcing) "bonding", is, necessarily, about self-transcendence. And right life is also, when founded on most profound self-understanding, a philosophical or religious process that is primarily moved by the Impulse to Realize Real God, or Truth, or Reality, or Divine Liberation. All else is a naive, self-indulgent, and absurd enterprise, based on egoity and immaturity.

Part Four of *Eleutherios*, "On Liberation from ego <u>and</u> egoic Society, or, Cooperation + Tolerance = Peace", is a Prophetic Essay by Ruchira Avatar Adi Da, Calling for an immediate global transformation of human politics and society. As Avatar Adi Da explains:

It may sound naive to speak of the necessity for the present (childish, and brutishly adolescent) crowd of governments and institutions to understand themselves and renounce the self-imagery and the techniques of enemies, but the feeling that it is naive to speak in such terms is *merely a reflection of egoic frustration and despair. Human beings everywhere must <u>now</u> transcend that very frustration and despair if they are going to prevent the enslavement and destruction of mankind.*

In Part Five of *Eleutherios*, "Cooperative, Human-Scale Community and the Integrity (Religious, and Altogether) of Civilization", Ruchira Avatar Adi Da Samraj lays out the practical steps that must be taken to reform human civilization and redirect it to the greater purposes of mankind.

Finally, in the extraordinary Epilogue, "I Have Come To Found A 'Bright' New Age Of Real-God-Man", Avatar Adi Da Reveals the Purpose of His Divine Descent in the world at this critical moment in history, and He Describes His unparalleled Vision of a most positive and benign future for humanity.

Eleutherios is Ruchira Avatar Adi Da's Invitation to you (and to all beings) to Realize Perfect Freedom by resort to His Divinely Liberating Grace. As Revealed in the subtitle of this magnificent Scripture, the Divine World-Teacher, Ruchira Avatar Adi Da Samraj, <u>Is</u> "The <u>Only</u> Truth That Sets the Heart Free".

Notes to
The Perfect Liberator

1. The Tantric traditions of India and the Himalayas describe as "heroic" the practice of an individual whose impulse to Liberation and commitment to his or her Guru are so strong that all circumstances of life, even those traditionally considered inauspicious for Spiritual practice (such as consumption of intoxicants and engagement in sexual activity), can be rightly made use of as part of the Spiritual process.

Avatar Adi Da's uniquely "Heroic" Ordeal, however, was undertaken not (primarily) for the sake of His own Liberation, but in order to discover, through His own experience, what is necessary for <u>all</u> beings to Realize the Truth. Because of His utter Freedom from egoic bondage and egoic karmas, Avatar Adi Da's Sadhana was "Heroic" in a manner that had never previously been possible and will never again be possible for any other being. As the Divine Person, it was necessary for Him to have experienced the entire gamut of human seeking, in order for Him to be able to Teach any and all that came to Him.

Avatar Adi Da has Instructed that, because of His unique "Heroic" Demonstration, His devotees can simply practice the Way He has Revealed and Given, and are not to attempt the (in any case impossible) task of duplicating His Ordeal.

2. See note 21, pp. 204-206.

3. See note 21, pp. 204-206.

4. See note 21, pp. 204-206.

5. For Avatar Adi Da's full discussion of His uniquely Complete Revelation in the context of the Great Tradition of mankind, see *The Seven Stages Of Life—The Seventeen Companions Of The True Dawn Horse, Book Ten: Transcending The Six Stages Of egoic Life, and Realizing The ego-Transcending Seventh Stage Of Life, In The Divine Way Of Adidam* ("'God'-Talk, Real-God-Realization, and Most Perfect Divine Awakening" and Epilogue) and *The Basket Of Tolerance—The Seventeen Companions Of The True Dawn Horse, Book Seventeen: The Perfect Guide To Perfectly <u>Unified</u> Understanding Of The One and Great Tradition Of Mankind, and Of The Divine Way Of Adidam As The Perfect <u>Completing</u> Of The One and Great Tradition Of Mankind* ("'God'-Talk, Real-God-Realization, and Most Perfect Divine Awakening"; "Ramana Maharshi's Realization and the Root-Center on the Right Side of the Heart"; and "The Unique Sixth Stage Foreshadowings of the Only-by-Me Revealed and Demonstrated and Given Seventh Stage of Life").

ELEUTHERIOS

(THE <u>ONLY</u> TRUTH THAT SETS THE HEART FREE)

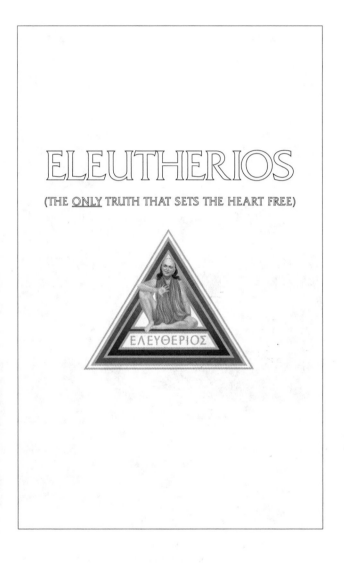

ΕΛΕΥΘΕΡΙΟΣ

RUCHIRA AVATAR ADI DA SAMRAJ
Adidam Samrajashram (Naitauba), Fiji, 1997

Do Not Misunderstand <u>Me</u>—
I Am <u>Not</u> "Within" <u>you</u>,
but you <u>Are</u> In <u>Me</u>,
and I Am <u>Not</u> a Mere "Man"
in the "Middle" of Mankind,
but All of Mankind Is Surrounded,
and Pervaded, and Blessed By <u>Me</u>

This Essay has been written by Avatar Adi Da Samraj as His Personal Introduction to each volume of His "Source-Texts". Its purpose is to help you to understand His great Confessions rightly, and not interpret His Words from a conventional point of view, as limited cultic statements made by an ego. His Description of what "cultism" really is is an astounding and profound Critique of mankind's entire religious, scientific, and social search. In "First Word", Avatar Adi Da is directly inviting you to inspect and relinquish the ego's motive to glorify itself and to refuse What is truly Great. Only by understanding this fundamental ego-fault can one really receive the Truth that Adi Da Samraj Reveals in this Book and in His Wisdom-Teaching altogether. And it is because this fault is so engrained and so largely unconscious that Avatar Adi Da has placed "First Word" at the beginning of each of His "Source-Texts", so that, each time you begin to read one of His twenty-three "Source-Texts", you may be refreshed and strengthened in your understanding of the right orientation and approach to Him and His Heart-Word.

Yes! There is <u>no</u> religion, <u>no</u> Way of God, <u>no</u> Way of Divine Realization, <u>no</u> Way of Enlightenment, and <u>no</u> Way of Liberation that is Higher or Greater than Truth Itself. Indeed, there is <u>no</u> religion, <u>no</u> science, <u>no</u> man or woman, <u>no</u> conditionally manifested being of any kind,

<u>no</u> world (<u>any</u> "where"), and <u>no</u> "God" (or "God"-Idea) that is Higher or Greater than Truth Itself.

Therefore, <u>no</u> ego-"I"[1] (or presumed separate, and, necessarily, actively separative, and, at best, only Truth-<u>seeking</u>, being or "thing") is (it<u>self</u>) Higher or Greater than Truth Itself. And <u>no</u> ego-"I" is (it<u>self</u>) even Equal to Truth Itself. And no ego-"I" is (it<u>self</u>) even (now, or ever) <u>Able</u> to Realize Truth Itself—because, necessarily, Truth (Itself) Inherently Transcends (or <u>Is</u> That Which <u>Is</u> Higher and Greater than) <u>every</u> one (him<u>self</u> or her<u>self</u>) and <u>every</u> "thing" (it<u>self</u>). Therefore, it is <u>only</u> in the transcending (or the "radical"[2] Process of Going Beyond the root, the cause, and the act) of egoity it<u>self</u> (or of presumed separateness, and of performed separativeness, and of even <u>all</u> ego-based seeking for Truth Itself) that Truth (Itself) <u>Is</u> Realized (<u>As</u> It <u>Is</u>, Utterly Beyond the ego-"I" it<u>self</u>).

Truth (Itself) <u>Is</u> That Which Is Always Already The Case. That Which <u>Is</u> The Case (Always, and Always Already) <u>Is</u> (necessarily) Reality. Therefore, Reality (Itself) <u>Is</u> Truth, and Reality (Itself) Is the <u>Only</u> Truth.

Reality (Itself) <u>Is</u> the <u>Only</u>, and, necessarily, Non-Separate, or All-and-all-Including, <u>and</u> All-and-all-Transcending, One and "What" That <u>Is</u>. Because It <u>Is</u> All and all, and because It <u>Is</u> (Also) <u>That</u> Which Transcends (or <u>Is</u> Higher and Greater than) All and all, Reality (Itself), Which <u>Is</u> Truth (Itself), or That Which Is The Case (Always, and Always Already), <u>Is</u> the One and Only <u>Real</u> God. Therefore, Reality (Itself) Is (necessarily) the One and Great Subject of true religion, and Reality (<u>Itself</u>) <u>Is</u> (necessarily) the One and Great Way of <u>Real</u> God, <u>Real</u> (and True) Divine Realization, <u>Real</u> (and, necessarily, Divine) En-Light-enment, and <u>Real</u> (and, necessarily, Divine) Liberation (from all egoity, all separateness, all separativeness, all fear, and all heartlessness).

Notes to *First Word* can be found on pp. 64-67.

The <u>only</u> true religion is the religion that <u>Realizes</u> Truth. The <u>only</u> true science is the science that <u>Knows</u> Truth. The <u>only</u> true man or woman (or being of any kind) is one that <u>Surrenders</u> to Truth. The only true world is one that <u>Embodies</u> Truth. And the only True (and <u>Real</u>) God Is the One Reality (or Condition of Being) That <u>Is</u> Truth. Therefore, <u>Reality</u> (Itself), Which Is the One and Only Truth, and (therefore, necessarily) the One and Only Real God, <u>must</u> become (or be made) the constantly applied Measure of religion, and of science, and of the world itself, and of even <u>all</u> of the life (and <u>all</u> of the mind) of Man—or else religion, and science, and the world itself, and even any and every sign of Man <u>inevitably</u> (all, and together) become a pattern of illusions, a mere (and even terrible) "problem", the very (and even principal) cause of human seeking, and the perpetual cause of contentious human strife. Indeed, if religion, and science, and the world itself, and the total life (and the total mind) of Man are not Surrendered and Aligned to Reality (Itself), and, Thus, Submitted to be Measured (or made Lawful) by Truth (Itself), and, Thus, Given to the truly devotional (and, thereby, truly ego-transcending) Realization of <u>That</u> Which Is the <u>Only</u> <u>Real</u> God—then, in the presumed "knowledge" of mankind, Reality (Itself), and Truth (Itself), and <u>Real</u> God (or the One and Only Existence, or Being, or Person That <u>Is</u>) <u>ceases</u> <u>to</u> <u>Exist</u>.

Aham Da Asmi.[3] Beloved, I <u>Am</u> Da, the One and Only Person Who <u>Is</u>, the Eternally Self-Existing, and Eternally Self-Radiant,[4] or "Bright",[5] Person of Love-Bliss, the One and Only and (necessarily) Divine Self (or Inherently Non-Separate, and, therefore, Inherently egoless, Self-Condition and Source-Condition) of one and of all and of All. I Am Self-Manifesting (now, and forever hereafter) <u>As</u> the Ruchira Avatar, Adi Da Samraj. I <u>Am</u> the Ruchira Avatar, Adi Da Samraj, the Avataric Realizer, the Avataric Revealer, the Avataric Incarnation, and the Avataric Revelation of Reality <u>Itself</u>.[6] I <u>Am</u> the Avatarically Incarnate Realizer, the

45

Avatarically Incarnate Revealer, and the Avatarically Incarnate Revelation of the One and Only Reality, Which Is the One and Only Truth, and Which Is the One and Only <u>Real</u> God. I <u>Am</u> the Great Realizer, Revealer, and Revelation long-Promised (and long-Expected) for the "late-time", <u>this</u> (now, and forever hereafter) time, the "dark" epoch of mankind's "Great Forgetting"[7] (and, <u>potentially</u>, the Great Epoch of mankind's Perpetual Remembering) of Reality, of Truth, of Real God, Which Is the Great, True, and Spiritual Divine Person (or the One and Non-Separate and Indivisible Source-Condition and Self-Condition) of all and All.

Beloved, I <u>Am</u> Da, the Divine Giver, the Giver (of All That I <u>Am</u>) to one and to all and to the All of all—now, and forever hereafter, here, and every "where" in the Cosmic domain. Therefore, for the Purpose of Revealing the Way of <u>Real</u> God, or of Real and True Divine Realization, and in order to Divinely En-Light-en and Divinely Liberate all and All, I Am (Uniquely, Completely, and Most Perfectly[8]) Revealing My Divine and Very Person (and "Bright" Self-Condition) to all and All, by Means of My Divine Self-Manifestation, <u>As</u> (and by Means of) the Ruchira Avatar, Adi Da Samraj.

In My Divine Self-Manifestation As the Ruchira Avatar, Adi Da Samraj, I <u>Am</u> the Divine Secret, the Divine Revelation of the <u>Esoteric</u> Truth, the Direct, and all-Completing, and all-Unifying Revelation of <u>Real</u> God.

My Divine Self-Confessions and My Divine Teaching-Revelations Are <u>the</u> Great (Final, and all-Completing, and all-Unifying) <u>Esoteric</u> Revelation to mankind, and <u>not</u> a merely <u>exoteric</u>, or conventionally religious, or even ordinary Spiritual, or ego-made, or so-called "cultic", communication to public (or merely social) ears.

The greatest opportunity, and the greatest responsibility, of My devotees is Satsang[9] with Me, Which is to live in the Condition of self-surrendering, self-forgetting, and, always more and more, self-transcending devotional relationship to Me, and, Thus and Thereby, to Realize the

Condition of the Divine Heart, the Condition of the Divine Person, Which Is the Divine and Non-Separate Self-Condition, and Source-Condition, of all and All, and Which Is Self-Existing and Self-Radiant Consciousness Itself, but Which is not separate in or as any one (or any "thing") at all. Therefore, My essential Gift to one and all is this Satsang with Me. And My essential Work with one and all is Satsang-Work, to Live (and to Be Merely Present) As the Divine Heart among My devotees.

The only-by-Me Revealed and Given Way of Adidam (Which is the only-by-Me Revealed and Given Way of the Heart, or the only-by-Me Revealed and Given Way of "Radical Understanding"[10]) is the Way of Satsang with Me—the devotionally Me-recognizing[11] and devotionally to-Me-responding practice (and ego-transcending self-discipline) of living in My constant Divine Company, such that the relationship with Me becomes the Real (and constant) Condition of life. Fundamentally, this Satsang with Me is the one thing done by My devotees. Because the only-by-Me Revealed and Given Way of Adidam is always (in every present-time moment) a directly ego-transcending and Really Me-Finding practice, the otherwise constant (and burdensome) tendency to seek is not exploited in this Satsang with Me. And the essential work of the community of the four formal congregations of My devotees[12] is to make ego-transcending Satsang with Me available to all others.

Everything that serves the availability of Satsang with Me is (now, and forever hereafter) the responsibility of the four formal congregations of My formally practicing devotees. I am not here to publicly "promote" this Satsang with Me. In the intimate circumstances of their humanly expressed devotional love of Me, I Speak My Divinely Self-Revealing Word to My devotees, and they (because of their devotional response to Me) bring My Divinely Self-Revealing Word to all others. Therefore, even though I am not (and have never been, and never will be) a "public"

Teacher (or a broadly publicly active, and conventionally socially conformed, "religious figure"), My devotees function fully and freely (<u>as</u> My devotees) in the daily public world of ordinary life.

I Always Already Stand Free. Therefore, I have always (in My Avataric-Incarnation-Work) Stood Free, in the traditional "Crazy" (and non-conventional, or spontaneous and non-"public") Manner,[13] in order to Guarantee the Freedom, the Uncompromising Rightness, and the Fundamental Integrity of My Teaching (Work and Word), and in order to Freely and Fully and Fully Effectively Perform My universal Blessing Work. I Am Present (now, and forever hereafter) to Divinely Serve, Divinely En-Light-en, and Divinely Liberate those who accept the Eternal Vow and <u>all</u> the life-responsibilities (or the full and complete practice)[14] associated with the only-by-Me Revealed and Given Way of Adidam. Because I Am Thus Given to My formally and fully practicing devotees, I do not Serve a "public" role, and I do not Work in a "public" (or even a merely "institutionalized") manner. Nevertheless, now, and forever hereafter, I <u>constantly</u> Bless <u>all</u> beings, and this <u>entire</u> world, and the <u>total</u> Cosmic domain. And <u>all</u> who feel My universally Given Blessing, and who recognize Me with true devotional love, are (Thus) Called to resort to Me, but only if they approach Me in the traditional devotional manner, as responsibly practicing (and truly ego-surrendering, and rightly Me-serving) members (or, in some, unique, cases, as invited guests) of one or the other of the four formal congregations of My formally practicing devotees.

I expect this formal discipline of right devotional approach to Me to have been freely and happily embraced by every one who would enter into My Company. The natural human reason for this is that there is a potential liability inherent in <u>all</u> human associations. And the root and nature of that potential liability is the <u>ego</u>, or the active human presumption of separateness, and the ego-act of human separativeness. Therefore, in order that the liabilities of egoity are understood, and voluntarily and responsibly disciplined, by those who approach Me, I require demonstrated right devotion, based on really effective self-understanding and truly heart-felt recognition-response to Me, as the basis for any one's right to enter into My Company. And, in this manner, not only the egoic tendency, but also the tendency toward religious "cultism", is constantly undermined in the only-by-Me Revealed and Given Way of Adidam.

Because people appear within this human condition, this simultaneously attractive and frightening "dream" world, they tend to live (and to interpret <u>both</u> the conditional, or cosmic and psycho-physical, reality <u>and</u> the Unconditional, or Divine, Reality) from the "point of view" of this apparent, and bewildering, mortal human condition. And, because of this universal human bewilderment, and the ongoing human reaction to the threatening force of mortal life-events, there is an even ancient ritual that <u>all</u> human beings rather unconsciously (or automatically, and without discriminative understanding) desire and tend to repeatedly (and under <u>all</u> conditions) enact. Therefore, wherever you see an association of human beings gathered for <u>any</u> purpose (or around <u>any</u> idea, or symbol, or person, or subject of any kind), the same human bewilderment-ritual is <u>tending</u> to be enacted by one and all.

Human beings <u>always</u> <u>tend</u> to encircle (and, thereby, to contain, and, ultimately, to entrap and abuse, or even to blithely ignore) the presumed "center" of their lives—a book, a person, a symbol, an idea, or whatever. They tend to encircle the "center" (or the "middle"), and they tend to seek to <u>exclusively</u> acquire all "things" (or all power of control) for the circle (or toward the "middle") of <u>themselves</u>. In this manner, the <u>group</u> becomes an <u>ego</u> ("inward"-directed, or separate and separative)—just as the individual body-mind becomes, by self-referring self-contraction, the separate and separative ego-"I" ("inward"-

directed, or ego-centric, and exclusively acquiring all "things", or all power of control, for itself). Thus, by <u>self-contraction</u> upon the presumed "center" of their lives, human beings, in their collective ego-centricity, make "cults" (or bewildered and frightened "centers" of power, and control, and exclusion) in <u>every</u> area of life.

Anciently, the "cult"-making process was done, most especially, in the political and social sphere—and religion was, as even now, mostly an exoteric, or political and social, exercise that was <u>always</u> used to legitimize (or, otherwise, to "de-throne") political and social "authority-figures". Anciently, the cyclically (or even annually) culminating product of this exoteric religio-political "cult" was the ritual "de-throning" (or ritual deposition) of the one in the "middle" (just as, even in these times, political leaders are periodically "deposed", by elections, by rules of term and succession, by scandal, by slander, by force, and so on).

Traditional societies, everywhere throughout the ancient world, made and performed this annual (or otherwise periodic) religio-political "cult" ritual. The ritual of "en-throning" and "de-throning" was a reflection of the human observation of the annual cycle of the seasons of the natural world, and the same ritual was a reflection of the human concern and effort to <u>control</u> the signs potential in the cycle of the natural world, in order to ensure human survival (through control of weather, harvests and every kind of "fate", or even every fraction of existence upon which human beings depend for both survival and pleasure, or psycho-physical well-being). Indeed, the motive behind the ancient agrarian (and, later, urbanized, or universalized) ritual of the one in the "middle" was, essentially, the same motive that, in the modern era, takes the form of the culture of scientific materialism (and even all of the modern culture of materialistic "realism")—it is the motive to gain, and to maintain, <u>control</u>, and the effort to control even everything and everyone (via both knowledge and gross power). Thus, the ritualized (or bewildered yes/no, or desire/fear) life of mankind in the modern era is, essentially, the same as that of mankind in the ancient days.

In the ancient ritual of "en-throning" and "de-throning", the person (or subject) in the "middle" was ritually mocked, abused, deposed, and banished—and a new person (or subject) was installed in the "center" of the religio-political "cult". In the equivalent modern ritual of dramatized ambiguity relative to everything and everyone (and, perhaps especially, "authority-figures"), the person (or symbol, or idea) in the "middle" (or that which is given power by means of popular fascination) is first "cultified" (or made much of), and then, progressively, doubted, mocked, and abused, until, at last, all the negative emotions are (by culturally and socially ritualized dramatization) dissolved, the "middle" (having thus ceased to be fascinating) is abandoned, and a "new" person (or symbol, or idea) becomes the subject of popular fascination (only to be reduced, eventually, to the same "cultic" ritual, or cycle of "rise" and "fall").

Just as in <u>every</u> other area of human life, the tendency of <u>all</u> those who, in the modern era, would become involved in religious or Spiritual life is also to make a "cult", a circle that ever increases its separate and separative dimensions, beginning from the "center", surrounding it, perhaps even, ultimately, controlling it to the degree that it altogether ceases to be effective (or even interesting). Such "cultism" is ego-based, and ego-reinforcing, and, no matter how "esoteric" it presumes itself to be, it is (as in the ancient setting) entirely exoteric, or, at least, more and more limited to (and by) merely social and gross physical activities and conditions.

The form that every "cult" imitates is the pattern of egoity (or the ego-"I") itself, the presumed "middle" of every ordinary individual life. It is the self-contraction, the avoidance of relationship, which "creates" the fearful sense of separate mind, and all the endless habits and motives of egoic desire, or bewildered (and self-deluded) seeking. It is what is, ordinarily, called (or presumed to be) the real and necessary and only "life".

From birth, the human being (by reaction to the blows and limits of psycho-physical existence) begins to presume separate existence to be his or her very nature, and, on that basis, the human individual spends his or her entire life generating and serving a circle of ownership (or self-protecting acquisition) all around the ego-"I". The egoic motive encloses all the other beings it can acquire, all the "things" it can acquire, all the states and thoughts it can acquire—<u>all</u> the possible emblems, symbols, experiences, and sensations it can possibly acquire. Therefore, when any human being begins to involve himself or herself in some religious or Spiritual association, or, for that matter, <u>any</u> extension of his or her own subjectivity, he or she tends again to "create" that same circle about a "center".

The "cult" (whether of religion, or of politics, or of science, or of popular culture) is a dramatization of egoity, of separativeness, even of the entrapment and betrayal of the "center" (or the "middle"), by one and all. Therefore, I have always Refused to assume the role and the position of the "man in the middle"—and I have always, from the beginning of My formal Teaching and Blessing Work, Criticized, Resisted, and Shouted About the "cultic" (or ego-based, and ego-reinforcing, and merely "talking" and "believing", and not understanding and not really practicing) "school" (or tendency) of ordinary religious and Spiritual life. Indeed, true Satsang with Me (or the true devotional relationship to Me) is an always (and specifically, and intensively) anti-"cultic", or truly non-"cultic", Process.

The true devotional relationship to Me is not separative, or merely "inward"-directed, nor is It about attachment to Me as a mere (and, necessarily, limited) human being (or a "man in the middle")—for, if My devotee indulges in ego-bound (or self-referring and self-serving) attachment to Me as a mere human "other", My Divine Nature (and, therefore, the Divine Nature of Reality Itself) is not (as the very Basis for religious and Spiritual practice in My Company) truly devotionally recognized and rightly devotionally acknowledged, and, if such non-recognition of Me is the case, there is no truly ego-transcending devotional response to My Divine Presence and Person, and, thus, such presumed-to-be "devotion" to Me is not Divine Communion, and such presumed-to-be "devotion" to Me is not Divinely Liberating. Therefore, because the true devotional (and, thus, truly devotionally Me-recognizing and truly devotionally to-Me-responding) relationship to Me is entirely a counter-egoic (and truly and only Divine) discipline, It does not tend to become a "cult" (or, otherwise, to support the "cultic" tendency of Man).

The true devotional practice of true Satsang with Me is (inherently) expansive, or relational, and the self-contracting (or separate and separative) self-"center" is neither Its motive nor Its source. In true Satsang with Me, the egoic "center" is always already undermined as a "center" (or a presumed separate, and actively separative, entity). The Principle of true Satsang with Me is Me, Beyond (and not "within", or otherwise supporting) the ego-"I".

True Satsang with Me is the true "Round Dance" of Esoteric Spirituality. I am not trapped in the "middle" of My devotees. I "Dance" in the "Round" with each and every one of My devotees. I "Dance" in the circle, and, therefore, I am not merely a "motionless man" in the "middle". At the true "Center" (or the Divine Heart), I Am— Beyond definition (or separateness). I Am the Indivisible (or Most Perfectly Prior, Inherently Non-Separate, Inherently egoless, or centerless, boundless, and, necessarily, Divine) Consciousness (Itself) and the Indivisible (or Most Perfectly Prior, Inherently Non-Separate, Inherently egoless, or centerless, boundless, and, necessarily, Divine) Light (Itself). I Am the Very Being and the Very Presence (or Self-Radiance) of Self-Existing and Eternally Unqualified (or Non-"Different"[15]) Consciousness (Itself).

In the "Round Dance" of true Satsang with Me (or of

right and true devotional relationship to Me), I (My Self) Am Communicated directly to every one who lives in heart-felt relationship with Me (insofar as each one feels, <u>Beyond</u> the ego-"I" of body-mind, to <u>Me</u>). Therefore, I am not the mere "man" (or the separate human, or psycho-physical, one), and I am not merely "in the middle" (or separated out, and limited, and confined, by egoic seekers). I <u>Am</u> the One (and all-Transcending) Person of Reality Itself, Non-Separate, never merely at the egoic "center" (or "in the middle", or "<u>within</u>", and "inward" to, the egoic body-mind of My any devotee), but always <u>with</u> each one (and all), and always in relationship with each one (and all), and always Beyond each one (and all).

Therefore, My devotee is not Called, by Me, merely to turn "inward" (or upon the ego-"I"), or to struggle and seek to survive merely as a self-contracted and self-referring and self-seeking and self-serving ego-"center". Instead, I Call My devotee to turn the heart (and the total body-mind) <u>toward</u> Me (all-and-All-Surrounding, and all-and-All-Pervading), <u>in</u> <u>relationship</u>, <u>Beyond</u> the body-mind-self of My devotee (and <u>not</u> <u>merely</u> "<u>within</u>", or contained and containable "within" the separate, separative, and self-contracted domain of the body-mind-self, or the ego-"I", of My would-be devotee). I Call My devotee to function freely, My Light and My Person always (and under all circumstances) presumed and experienced (and not merely sought). Therefore, true Satsang with Me is the Real Company of Truth, or of Reality Itself (Which <u>Is</u> the Only Real God). True Satsang with Me Serves life, because I Move (or Radiate) into life. I always Contact life in relationship.

I do not Call My devotees to become absorbed into a "cultic" gang of exoteric and ego-centric religionists. I certainly Call <u>all</u> My devotees to cooperative community (or, otherwise, to fully cooperative collective and personal relationship) with one another—but <u>not</u> to do so in an egoic, separative, world-excluding, xenophobic, and intolerant manner. Rather, My devotees are Called, by Me, to

<u>transcend</u> <u>egoity</u> through <u>right</u> and <u>true</u> devotional rela-
tionship to Me, <u>and</u> mutually tolerant and peaceful cooperation with one another, <u>and</u> all-tolerating cooperative
and compassionate and all-loving and all-including relationship with <u>all</u> of mankind, and with even <u>all</u> beings.

I Give My devotees the "Bright" Force of My own
Divine Consciousness Itself, Whereby they can become
capable of "Bright" life. I Call for the devotion, but also
the intelligently discriminative self-understanding, the
rightly and freely living self-discipline, and the full functional capability, of My devotees. I do not Call My devotees to resist or eliminate life, or to strategically escape life,
or to identify with the world-excluding ego-centric
impulse. I Call My devotees to live a positively functional
life. I do not Call My devotees to separate themselves from
vital life, from vital enjoyment, from existence in the form
of human life. I Call for <u>all</u> the human life-functions to be
<u>really</u> and <u>rightly</u> known, and to be <u>really</u> and <u>rightly</u>
understood, and to be <u>really</u> and <u>rightly</u> lived (and not
reduced by or to the inherently bewildered, and inherently "cultic", or self-centered and fearful, "point of view"
of the separate and separative ego-"I"). I Call for <u>every</u>
human life-function to be revolved away from self-
contraction (or ego-"I"), and (by Means of that revolving
turn) to be turned "<u>outwardly</u>" (or expansively, or counter-
contractively) to all and All, and (thereby, and always
directly, or in an all-and-All-transcending manner) to <u>Me</u>—
rather than to be turned merely "<u>inwardly</u>" (or contractively, or counter-expansively), and, as a result, turned
away from <u>Me</u> (and from all and All). Thus, I Call for <u>every</u>
human life-function to be thoroughly (and life-positively,
and in the context of a fully participatory human life)
aligned and adapted to <u>Me</u>, and, Thus and Thereby, to be
turned and Given to the Realization of Truth (or Reality
Itself, Which <u>Is</u> the Only Real God).

Truly benign and positive life-transformations are the
characteristic signs of right, true, full, and fully devotional

Satsang with Me, and freely life-positive feeling-energy is the characteristic accompanying "mood" of right, true, full, and fully devotional Satsang with Me. The characteristic life-sign of right, true, full, and fully devotional Satsang with Me is the capability for self-transcending relatedness, based on the free disposition of no-seeking and no-dilemma. Therefore, the characteristic life-sign of right, true, full, and fully devotional Satsang with Me is not the tendency to seek some "other" condition. Rather, the characteristic life-sign of right, true, full, and fully devotional Satsang with Me is freedom from the presumption of dilemma within the present-time condition.

One who rightly, truly, fully, and fully devotionally understands My Words of Divine Self-Revelation and Divine Instruction, and whose life is lived in right, true, full, and fully devotional Satsang with Me, is not necessarily, in function or appearance, "different" from the ordinary (or natural) human being. Such a one has not, necessarily, acquired some special psychic abilities, or visionary abilities, and so on. The "radical" understanding (or root self-understanding) I Give to My devotees is not, itself, the acquisition of any particular "thing" of experience. My any particular devotee may, by reason of his or her developmental tendencies, experience (or precipitate) the arising of extraordinary psycho-physical abilities and extraordinary psycho-physical phenomena, but not necessarily. My every true devotee is simply Awakening (and always Awakened to Me) within the otherwise bewildering "dream" of ordinary human life.

Satsang with Me is a natural (or spontaneously, and not strategically, unfolding) Process, in Which the self-contraction that is each one's suffering is transcended by Means of total psycho-physical (or whole bodily) Communion with My Real (and Really, and tangibly, experienced) Divine (Spiritual, and Transcendental)[16] Presence and Person. My devotee is (as is the case with any and every ego-"I") always tending to be preoccupied with ego-based seeking, but, all the while of his or her life in <u>actively</u> self-surrendering (and really self-forgetting, and, more and more, self-transcending) devotional Communion with Me, I Am <u>Divinely</u> Attracting (and <u>Divinely</u> Acting upon) My true devotee's heart (and total body-mind), and (Thus and Thereby) Dissolving and Vanishing My true devotee's fundamental egoity (and even all of his or her otherwise motivating dilemma and seeking-strategy).

There are <u>two</u> principal tendencies by which I am always being confronted by My devotee. One is the tendency to <u>seek</u>, rather than to truly enjoy and to fully animate the Condition of Satsang with Me. And the other is the tendency to make a self-contracting circle around Me—and, thus, to make a "cult" of ego-"I" (and of the "man in the middle"), or to duplicate the ego-ritual of mere fascination, and of inevitable resistance, and of never-Awakening unconsciousness. Relative to these two tendencies, I Give <u>all</u> My devotees only <u>one</u> resort. It is this true Satsang, the devotionally Me-recognizing, and devotionally to-Me-responding, and always really counter-egoic devotional relationship to <u>Me</u>.

The Great Secret of My own Person, and of My Divine Blessing-Work (now, and forever hereafter), and, therefore, the Great Secret of the only-by-Me Revealed and Given Way of Adidam, Is that I am <u>not</u> the "man in the middle", but I <u>Am</u> Reality Itself, I <u>Am</u> the Only <u>One</u> Who <u>Is</u>, I <u>Am</u> That Which Is Always Already The Case, I <u>Am</u> the Non-Separate (and, necessarily, Divine) Person (or One and Very Self, or One and True Self-Condition) of all and All (<u>Beyond</u> the ego-"I" of every one, and of all, and of All).

Aham Da Asmi. Beloved, I <u>Am</u> Da, the One and Only and Non-Separate and Indivisible Divine Person, the Non-Separate and Indivisible Self-Condition and Source-Condition of all and All. I <u>Am</u> the "Bright" Person, the One and Only and Self-Existing and Self-Radiant Person, Who <u>Is</u> the One and Only and Non-Separate and Indivisible and Indestructible Light of All and all. I <u>Am</u> <u>That</u> One and Only and Non-Separate <u>One</u>. And, <u>As</u> <u>That</u> <u>One</u>, and <u>Only</u> <u>As</u> <u>That</u> <u>One</u>, I Call all human beings to recognize Me, and to respond to Me with right, true, and full devotion (by Means of formal practice of the only-by-Me Revealed and Given Way of Adidam).

I do not tolerate the so-called "cultic" (or ego-made, and ego-reinforcing) approach to Me. I do not tolerate the seeking ego's "cult" of the "man in the middle". I am not a self-deluded ego-man, making much of himself, and looking to include everyone-and-everything around himself for the sake of social and political power. To be the "man in the middle" is to be in a Man-made trap, an absurd mummery of "cultic" devices that enshrines and perpetuates the ego-"I" in one and all. Therefore, I do not make or tolerate the religion-making "cult" of ego-Man. I do not tolerate the inevitable abuses of religion, of Spirituality, of Truth Itself, and of My own Person (even in bodily human Form) that are made (in endless blows and mockeries) by ego-based mankind when the Great Esoteric Truth of devotion to the Adept-Realizer is not rightly understood and rightly practiced.

The Great Means for the Teaching, and the Blessing, and the Awakening, and the Divine Liberating of mankind (and of even all beings) Is the Adept-Realizer Who, by Virtue of True Divine Realization, Is Able to (and, indeed, cannot do otherwise than) Stand In and <u>As</u> the Divine (or Real and Inherent and One and Only) Position, and to <u>Be</u>, Thus and Thereby, the Divine Means (In Person) for the Divine Helping of one and all. This Great Means Is the Great Esoteric Principle of the collective historical Great Tradition[17] of mankind. And Such Adept-Realizers Are (in their Exercise of the Great Esoteric Principle) the Great Revelation-Sources That Are at the Core and Origin of <u>all</u> the right and true religious and Spiritual traditions within the collective historical Great Tradition of mankind.

By Means of My (now, and forever hereafter) Divinely Descended and Divinely "Emerging"[18] Avataric Incarnation, I Am the Ruchira Avatar, Adi Da Samraj—the Divine Heart-Master, the first, the last, and the only Adept-Realizer of the seventh (or Most Perfect, and all-Completing) stage of life.[19] I Am the Ruchira Avatar, Adi Da Samraj, the Avataric Incarnation (and Divine World-Teacher[20]) everywhere Promised for the "late-time" (or "dark" epoch)—which "late-time" (or "dark" epoch) is now upon all of mankind. I Am the Great and Only and Non-Separate and (necessarily) Divine Person, Appearing in Man-Form As the Ruchira Avatar, Adi Da Samraj, in order to Teach, and to Bless, and to Awaken, and to Divinely Liberate all of mankind (and even all beings, every "where" in the Cosmic domain). Therefore, by Calling every one and all (and All) to Me, I Call every one and all (and All) Only to the Divine Person, Which Is My own and Very Person (or Very Self, or Very Self-Condition), and Which Is Reality Itself, or Truth Itself, the Indivisible and Indestructible Light That Is the Only Real God, and Which Is the One and Very and Non-Separate and Only Self (or Self-Condition, and Source-Condition) of all and All (Beyond the ego-"I" of every one, and of all, and of All).

The only-by-Me Revealed and Given Way of Adidam necessarily (and As a Unique Divine Gift) requires and involves devotional recognition-response to Me In and Via (and As) My bodily (human) Avataric-Incarnation-Form. However, because I Call every one and all (and All) to Me Only As the Divine Person (or Reality Itself), the only-by-Me Revealed and Given Way of Adidam is not about ego, and egoic seeking, and the egoic (or the so-called "cultic") approach to Me (as the "man in the middle").

According to all the esoteric traditions within the collective historical Great Tradition of mankind, to devotionally approach any Adept-Realizer as if he or she is (or is limited to being, or is limited by being) a mere (or "ordinary", or even merely "extraordinary") human entity is the great "sin" (or fault), or the great error whereby the would-be devotee fails to "meet the mark". Indeed, the Single

Greatest Esoteric Teaching common to all the esoteric religious and Spiritual traditions within the collective historical Great Tradition of mankind Is that the Adept-Realizer should always and only (and only devotionally) be recognized and approached As the Embodiment and the Real Presence of That (Reality, or Truth, or Real God) Which would be Realized (Thus and Thereby) by the devotee.

Therefore, no one should misunderstand Me. By Revealing and Confessing My Divine Status to one and all and All, I am not indulging in self-appointment, or in illusions of grandiose Divinity. I am not claiming the "Status" of the "Creator-God" of exoteric (or public, and social, and idealistically pious) religion. Rather, by Standing Firm in the Divine Position (As I Am), and, Thus and Thereby, Refusing to be approached as a mere man, or as a "cult"-figure, or as a "cult"-leader, or to be in any sense defined (and, thereby, trapped, and abused, or mocked) as the "man in the middle", I Am Demonstrating the Most Perfect Fulfillment (and the Most Perfect Integrity, and the Most Perfect Fullness) of the Esoteric, and Most Perfectly Non-Dual, Realization of Reality. And, by Revealing and Giving the Way of Adidam, Which Is the Way of ego-transcending devotion to Me As the One and Only and Non-Separate and (necessarily) Divine Person, I Am (with Most Perfect Integrity, and Most Perfect Fullness) Most Perfectly (and in an all-Completing and all-Unifying Manner) Fulfilling the Primary Esoteric Tradition (and the Great Esoteric Principle) of the collective historical Great Tradition of mankind—Which Primary Esoteric Tradition and Great Esoteric Principle Is the Tradition and the Principle of devotion to the Adept-Realizer As the Very Person and the Direct (or Personal Divine) Helping-Presence of the Eternal and Non-Separate Divine Self-Condition and Source-Condition of all and All.

Whatever (or whoever) is cornered (or trapped on all sides) bites back (and fights, or seeks, to break free). Whatever (or whoever) is "in the middle" (or limited and "centered" by attention) is patterned by (or conformed to) the ego-"I" (and, if objectified as "other", is forced to represent the ego-"I", and is even made a scapegoat for the pains, the sufferings, the powerless ignorance, and the abusive hostility of the ego-"I").

If there is no escape (or no Way out) of the corner (or the "centered" trap) of ego-"I", the heart goes mad, and the body-mind becomes more and more "dark" (bereft of the Divine and Indivisible and Inherently Free Light of Love-Bliss).

I am not the "man in the middle". I do not stand here as a mere man, "middled" to the "center" (or the cornering trap) of ego-based mankind. I am not an ego-"I", or a mere "other", or the representation (and the potential scapegoat) of the ego-"I" of mankind (or of any one at all).

I <u>Am</u> the Indivisible and Non-Separate One, the One and Only and (necessarily) Divine Person—the Perfectly Subjective[21] Self-Condition (and Source-Condition) That Is Perfectly centerless, and Perfectly boundless, Eternally Beyond the "middle" of all and All, and Eternally Surrounding, Pervading, and Blessing all and All.

I <u>Am</u> the Way Beyond the self-cornering (and "other"-cornering) trap of ego-"I".

In this "late-time" (or "dark" epoch) of worldly ego-Man, the collective of mankind is "darkened" (and cornered) by egoity. Therefore, mankind has become mad, Lightless, and, like a cornered "thing", aggressively hostile in its universally competitive fight and bite.

Therefore, I have not Come here merely to stand Manly in the "middle" of mankind, to suffer its biting abuses, or even to be coddled and ignored in a little corner of religious "cultism".

I have Come here to Divinely Liberate one and all (and All) from the "dark" culture and effect of this "late-time", and (now, and forever hereafter) to Divinely Liberate one and all (and All) from the pattern and the act of ego-"I", and (Most Ultimately) to Divinely Translate[22] one and all (and All) Into the Indivisible, Perfectly Subjective, and Eternally Non-Separate Self-Domain of the Divine Love-Bliss-Light.

The ego-"I" is a "centered" (or separate and separative) trap, from which the heart (and even the entire body-mind) must be Retired. I Am the Way (or the Very Means) of that Retirement from egoity. I Refresh the heart (and even the entire body-mind) of My devotee, in every moment My devotee resorts to Me (by devotionally recognizing Me, and devotionally, and ecstatically, and also, often, meditatively, responding to Me) Beyond the "middle", Beyond the "centering" act (or trapping gesture) of ego-"I" (or self-contraction).

I Am the Perfectly Subjective Self-Condition (and Source-Condition) of every one, and of all, and of All—but the Perfectly Subjective Self-Condition (and Source-Condition) is not "within" the ego-"I" (or separate and separative body-mind). The Perfectly Subjective Self-Condition (and Source-Condition) is not in the "center" (or the "middle") of Man (or of mankind). The Perfectly Subjective Self-Condition (and Source-Condition) of one, and of all, and of All Is Inherently centerless, or Always Already Beyond the self-contracted "middle", and to Be Found only "outside" (or by transcending) the bounds of separateness, relatedness, and "difference". Therefore, to Realize the Perfectly Subjective Self-Condition and Source-Condition (or the Perfectly Subjective, and, necessarily, Divine, Heart) of one, and of all, and of All (or even, in any moment, to exceed the ego-trap, and to be Refreshed at heart, and in the total body-mind), it is necessary to feel (and to, ecstatically, and even meditatively, swoon) Beyond the "center" (or Beyond the "point of view" of separate ego-"I" and separative body-mind). Indeed, Most Ultimately, it is only in self-transcendence to the degree of unqualified relatedness (and Most Perfect Divine Samadhi, or Utterly Non-Separate Enstasy) that the Inherently centerless and boundless Divine Self-Condition and Source-

Condition Stands Obvious and Free (and Is, Thus and Thereby, Most Perfectly Realized).

It Is only by Means of Me-recognizing (and to-Me-responding) devotional meditation on Me (and otherwise ecstatic heart-Contemplation of Me), and total, and totally open, and totally self-forgetting psycho-physical Reception of Me, that your madness of heart (and of body-mind) is (now, and now, and now) escaped, and your "darkness" is En-Light-ened (even, at last, Most Perfectly). Therefore, be My true devotee, and, by formally, and rightly, and truly, and fully, and fully devotionally practicing the only-by-Me Revealed and Given Way of Adidam (Which Is the True and Complete Way of the True and Real Divine Heart), always Find Me Beyond your self-"center" in every here and now.

Aham Da Asmi. Beloved, I Am Da. And, because I Am Infinitely and Non-Separately "Bright", all and All Are In My Sphere of "Brightness". By feeling and surrendering Into My Infinite Sphere of Divine Self-"Brightness", My every devotee Is In Me. And, Beyond his or her self-contracting and separative act of ego-"I", My every devotee (self-surrendered Into heart-Communion With Me) Is the One and Only and Non-Separate and Real God I Have Come to Serve, by Means of My Divine Descent, My Divine Avataric Incarnation, and My (now, and forever hereafter) Divine "Emergence" (here, and every "where" in the Cosmic domain).

Notes to
FIRST WORD

1. The ego-"I" is the fundamental self-contraction, or the sense of separate and separative existence.

2. See note 4, p. 199.

3. The Sanskrit phrase "Aham Da Asmi" means "I (Aham) Am (Asmi) Da". The Name "Da", meaning "the One Who Gives", indicates that Avatar Adi Da Samraj is the Supreme Divine Giver, the Avataric Incarnation of the Very Divine Person.

4. Avatar Adi Da uses "Self-Existing and Self-Radiant" to indicate the two fundamental aspects of the One Divine Person—Existence (or Being, or Consciousness) Itself, and Radiance (or Energy, or Light) Itself.

5. See note 8, p. 200.

6. This passage is Avatar Adi Da's Self-Confession as "Avatar". In Sanskrit, "Ruchira" means "bright, radiant, effulgent". Thus, the Reference "Ruchira Avatar" indicates that Avatar Adi Da Samraj is the "Bright" (or Radiant) Descent of the Divine Reality Itself (or the Divine Truth Itself, Which Is the Only Real God) into the conditional worlds, Appearing here in bodily (human) Form. Avatar Adi Da Samraj is the "Avataric Incarnation", or the Divinely Descended Embodiment, of the Divine Person. The reference "Avataric Incarnation" indicates that Avatar Adi Da Samraj fulfills both the traditional expectation of the East—that the True God-Man is an Avatar, or an utterly Divine "Descent" of Real God in conditionally manifested form—and the traditional expectations of the West—that the True God-Man is an Incarnation, or an utterly human Embodiment of Real God.

7. "The 'late-time', or 'dark' epoch" is a phrase that Avatar Adi Da uses to Describe the present era, in which doubt of God (and of anything at all beyond mortal existence) is more and more pervading the entire world, and in which the separate and separative ego-"I", which is the root of all suffering and conflict, is regarded to be the ultimate principle of life.

8. See note 14, p. 202.

9. The Hindi word "Satsang" literally means "true (or right) relationship", "the company of Truth". In the Way of Adidam, Satsang is the eternal relationship of mutual sacred commitment between Avatar Adi Da Samraj and each true and formally acknowledged practitioner of the Way of Adidam.

10. Avatar Adi Da uses "understanding" to mean "the process of transcending egoity". Thus, to "understand" is to simultaneously observe the activity of the self-contraction and to surrender that activity via devotional resort to Avatar Adi Da Samraj.

Avatar Adi Da has Revealed that, despite their intention to Realize Reality (or Truth, or Real God), all religious and Spiritual traditions (other than the Way of Adidam He has Revealed and Given) are involved, in one manner or another, with the search to satisfy the ego. Only Avatar Adi Da has Revealed the Way to "radically" understand the ego and (in due course, through intensive formal practice of the Way of Adidam, as His formally acknowledged devotee) to most perfectly transcend the ego. Thus, the Way Avatar Adi Da has Given is the "Way of 'Radical' Understanding".

11. The entire practice of the Way of Adidam is founded in heart-recognition of Ruchira Avatar Adi Da Samraj as the Very Divine Being in Person.

AVATAR ADI DA SAMRAJ: The only-by-Me Revealed and Given Way of Adidam (Which is the only-by-Me Revealed and Given Way of the Heart) is the Way of life you live when you rightly, truly, fully, and fully devotionally recognize Me, and when, on that basis, you rightly, truly, fully, and fully devotionally respond to Me.

. . . In responsive devotional recognition of Me, the principal faculties are loosed from the objects to which they are otherwise bound— loosed from the patterns of self-contraction. The faculties turn to Me, and, in that turning, there is tacit recognition of Me, tacit experiential Realization of Me, of Happiness Itself, of My Love-Bliss-Full Condition. That "Locating" of Me opens the body-mind spontaneously. When you have been thus Initiated by Me, it then becomes your responsibility, your sadhana, to continuously Remember Me, to constantly return to this recognition of Me, in which you are Attracted to Me, in which you respond to Me spontaneously with all the principal faculties. ("Recognize My Divine Body and 'Bright' Person, and Let Everything Melt That Is 'Between' You and Me", in *Hridaya Rosary*)

12. See pp. 220-31 for a description of the congregations of Adidam.

13. The Adepts of what Avatar Adi Da calls "the 'Crazy Wisdom' tradition" (of which He is the supreme, seventh stage exemplar) are Realizers of the fourth, fifth, or sixth stages of life in any culture or time who, through spontaneous Free action, blunt Wisdom, and liberating laughter, shock or humor people into self-critical awareness of their egoity, which is a prerequisite for receiving the Realizer's Spiritual Transmission. Typically, such Realizers manifest "Crazy" activity only

occasionally or temporarily, and never for its own sake but only as "skillful means".

Avatar Adi Da Himself has always addressed the ego in a unique "Crazy-Wise" manner, theatrically dramatizing, and poking fun at, the self-contracted habits, predilections, and destinies of His devotees. His "Crazy-Wise" Manner is a Divine Siddhi, an inherent aspect of His Avataric Incarnation. Through His "Crazy-Wise" Speech and Action, Avatar Adi Da Penetrates the being and loosens the patterns of ego-bondage (individually and collectively) in His devotees. The "Shock" of Truth Delivered via His "Crazy Wisdom" humbles and opens the heart, making way for the deeper reception of His Spiritual Blessing.

14. For a description of the Vow and responsibilities associated with the Way of Adidam, see pp. 219-39.

15. "Difference" is the epitome of the egoic presumption of separateness—in contrast with the Realization of Oneness, or Non-"Difference", that is native to Spiritual and Transcendental Divine Self-Consciousness.

16. Avatar Adi Da uses the terms "Spiritual", "Transcendental", and "Divine" in reference to different dimensions of Reality that are Realized progressively in the Way of Adidam. "Spiritual" refers to the reception of the Spirit-Force (in the "basic" and "advanced" contexts of the fourth stage of life and in the context of the fifth stage of life); "Transcendental" refers to the Realization of Consciousness Itself as separate from the world (in the context of the sixth stage of life); and "Divine" refers to the Most Perfect Realization of Consciousness Itself as utterly Non-separate from the world (in the context of the seventh stage of life). (See also note 21, pp. 204-206.)

17. The "Great Tradition" is Avatar Adi Da's term for the total inheritance of human, cultural, religious, magical, mystical, Spiritual, and Transcendental paths, philosophies, and testimonies from all the eras and cultures of humanity, which inheritance has (in the present era of worldwide communication) become the common legacy of mankind. Avatar Adi Da Samraj is the seventh stage, or Divine, Fulfillment of the Great Tradition.

18. On January 11, 1986, Avatar Adi Da passed through a profound Yogic Swoon, which He later Described as the initial Event of His Divine "Emergence". Avatar Adi Da's Divine "Emergence" is an ongoing Process in which His bodily (human) Form has been (and is ever more profoundly and potently being) conformed to Himself, the Very Divine Person, such that His bodily (human) Form is now (and forever hereafter) an utterly Unobstructed Sign and Agent of His own Divine Being.

19. For Avatar Adi Da's extended Instruction relative to the seven stages of life, see *The Seven Stages Of Life—The Seventeen Companions Of The True Dawn Horse, Book Ten: Transcending The Six Stages Of egoic Life, and Realizing The ego-Transcending Seventh Stage Of Life, In The Divine Way Of Adidam.* (See also note 21, pp. 204-206.)

20. Avatar Adi Da Samraj is the Divine World-Teacher because His Wisdom-Teaching is the uniquely Perfect Instruction to every being— in this (and every) world—in the total process of Divine Enlightenment. Furthermore, Avatar Adi Da Samraj constantly Extends His Regard to the entire world (and the entire Cosmic domain)—not on the political or social level, but as a Spiritual matter, constantly Working to Bless and Purify all beings everywhere.

21. Avatar Adi Da uses "Perfectly Subjective" to Describe the True Divine Source, or "Subject", of the conditional world—as opposed to the conditions, or "objects", of experience. Thus, in the phrase "Perfectly Subjective", the word "Subjective" does not have the sense of "relating to the merely phenomenal experience, or the arbitrary presumptions, of an individual", but, rather, it has the sense of "relating to Consciousness Itself, the True Subject of all apparent experience".

22. In the context of Divine Enlightenment in the seventh stage of life in the Way of Adidam, the Spiritual process continues. Avatar Adi Da has uniquely Revealed the four phases of the seventh stage process: Divine Transfiguration, Divine Transformation, Divine Indifference, and Divine Translation.

Divine Translation is the most ultimate "Event" of the entire process of Divine Awakening. Avatar Adi Da Describes Divine Translation as the Outshining of all noticing of objective conditions, through the infinitely magnified Force of Consciousness Itself. Divine Translation is the Outshining of all destinies, wherein there is no return to the conditional realms.

For Avatar Adi Da's extended Discussion of Divine Translation, see *The All-Completing and Final Divine Revelation To Mankind— The Seventeen Companions Of The True Dawn Horse, Book Eleven: A Summary Description Of The Supreme Yoga Of The Seventh Stage Of Life In The Divine Way Of Adidam, Part Two,* or *The Dawn Horse Testament Of The Ruchira Avatar,* chapter forty-four.

RUCHIRA AVATAR ADI DA SAMRAJ
Adidam Samrajashram (Naitauba), Fiji, 1997

Eleutherios
(The <u>Only</u> Truth That Sets the Heart Free)

I
Eleutherios

ONE

Truth is the Ultimate Form (or the Inherently Perfect State) of "Knowledge" (if mere knowledge becomes Truth-Realization).

Truth is That Which, when fully Realized (and, Thus, "Known", even via the transcending of <u>all</u> conditional knowledge and <u>all</u> conditional experience), sets you Free from <u>all</u> bondage and <u>all</u> seeking.

Truth is Eleutherios,[1] the Perfect Liberator.

Notes to the Text of *Eleutherios* appear on pp. 199-213.

TWO

Real God is not the awful Creator, the world-making and ego-making Titan, the Nature-"God" of worldly theology. Real God is not the First Cause, the Ultimate Other, or any of the Objective Ideas of mind-made philosophy. Real God is not any Image created (and defined) by the religious ego. Real God is not any Power contacted (and limited) by the mystical or the scientific ego. Real God is not any Goal that motivates the social ego.

Real God is Truth, or That Which, when Perfectly "Known" (or fully Realized), sets you entirely Free.

Real God is Eleutherios, the Perfect Liberator.

THREE

Real God is not, in Truth, the Cause (or the Objective Origin) of the conditional world and the ego (or the apparently separate self-consciousness). All causes (including any Ultimate Objective Cause) are only conditional modifications of conditional Nature.

Every cause is moving Energy, or the conditional mover of Energy. Therefore, the Ultimate Cause is, Itself, only Energy, or the Ultimate conditional mover of Energy. No cause, and no Cause of causes, is Truth Itself, since to know a cause (or the Cause) is merely to know an object (or the Object) and not to be liberated from bondage to the search for objective (or otherwise conditional) existence itself.

The knowledge of objects does not set you Free, since it is the knower (rather than the known) that knows itself to be bound. Freedom can only be Realized by transcending the subject (or knower) of conditional knowledge, not by increasing the objects of conditional knowledge. Therefore, Freedom is not Realized even in the attainment of an Ultimate Object of mere (or conditional) knowledge.

FOUR

Real God is <u>not</u> the Independent (or separate) <u>Cause</u> (or the <u>Objective</u>, or "Outside", Origin) of the world.

Real God is the Utterly Non-separate <u>Source</u> (or the <u>Perfectly Subjective</u>, and always already <u>As Is</u>, or Un-changing, Origin) of the world.

The presumed Cause of causes is not Truth, since to <u>be</u> a separate knower, and even to <u>know</u> such a Cause (or "Other"), does not (or cannot) set you Free from the knower (or the separate, and inherently separative, ego-"I"[2]) itself.

The experience of that which changes does not set you Free from the experiencer (or the separate, and inherently separative, ego-"I") itself.

Likewise, the experience, or the knowing, or even any kind of Realizing of causes, or of the presumed Cause of causes, does not (and cannot) set you Free from the separate (and inherently separative) ego-"I" (or psycho-physical self-contraction) itself.

<u>Only</u> the Realization of That Which Is always already The Case sets you Free from ego-"I" itself (and from <u>all</u> that is merely conditional, changing, separate, contracted, or "different"[3]).

Therefore, if you are to <u>Be</u> Free, the Perfectly Subjective (or Non-Objective, and Non-separate, or Non-"different") <u>Source</u> of the presumed Cause of causes, and the Perfectly Subjective (or Non-Objective, and Non-separate, or Non-"different") Source of <u>all</u> causes (and of <u>all</u> effects), must be "Known" (or, rather, Realized in Truth).

FIVE

The Existence of Real God is not proven (or even rightly affirmed) by appeal to the process of objective (or observable, or, otherwise, presumed) causation. But the Existence of Real God is (or, in due course, is Realized to be) Self-Evident (or Inherently Obvious) in the Real Process of Realizing the Perfectly Subjective Source of all causes, all effects, all seeking, all mere (or conditional) experience, all mere (or conditional) knowledge, and the conditional self-consciousness (or self-contracted ego-"I") that engages in causes, effects, seeking, mere (or conditional) experience, and mere (or conditional) knowledge. Therefore, the only "proof" (or right "affirmation") of the Existence of Real God is the Real, and "radical"[4] (or most direct, or Inherent, and not caused), and, Ultimately, Most Perfect, Realization of That Which always already Exists.

Consciousness (Itself) Is That Which always already Exists.

Consciousness (Itself) Is always already The Case, no matter what arises, and even if no "thing" arises.

Real God is Consciousness (<u>Itself</u>). Consciousness (Itself), or the Perfectly Subjective Source (and the Non-separate Self-Condition) of the apparent conditional world and the apparent conditional self, <u>Is</u> the only Real God.

The Deep Non-separate Space of Consciousness (Itself) is the Matrix in Which the Origin and the Ultimate (and, necessarily, Divine) Condition of conditional self, mind, body, world, the entire cosmos of conditional Nature, and the Universal Field of Energy is Inherently Obvious. When This (Deep Non-separate Space of Consciousness Itself) is "Known" (or fully Realized), the apparent conditional world and the apparent conditional self are fully "Known" (and, Thus, transcended) in the Realization of Truth.

To "Know" (or to Realize) Consciousness Itself <u>As</u> Real God (and, Thus, to "Know", or to Realize, Real God <u>As</u> Consciousness Itself, or <u>As</u> the Perfectly Subjective Source, and the Non-separate Self-Condition, of the conditional world and the conditional self) is to transcend both the conditional world and the conditional self by Means of Truth, or the only "Knowledge" (or Realization) That can set you Free.

SIX

Real God is not "Known" (or Realized) by the body (or in the process of bodily experience), since Real God is not reducible to any kind of object (or Objective Force).

Real God confronts you bodily, materially, or in the objective (or otherwise conditional) plane of conditional Nature only in the form of effects (or an Effective Influence). Therefore, Real God cannot be "Known" <u>As</u> Real God (or Truth) via any confrontation in the apparently objective (or otherwise conditional) realm of conditional Nature. Objective effects (including an Ultimate Objective Influence) are only conditional (or representative) forms of Real God. Therefore, bodily experience, or bodily confrontation with conditional Nature, does not prove, or even necessarily indicate (or point to), the Existence of Real God.

No bodily experience is an encounter with Truth.

No bodily experience can set you Free.

SEVEN

Real God is not an Object or an Image or an Idea that can confront the mind. Whatever confronts (or is known by) the mind only modifies and occupies the mind itself. Occupation with ideas, or states of mind, can only motivate you toward further activities of mind (and body). Therefore, there is no idea that <u>Is</u> Truth, since attention to an idea cannot liberate attention from mind itself.

EIGHT

𝔹odily experience and mental (or conditional) knowledge are both based on encounters with objects. In general, bodily experience and mental knowledge motivate you to seek more bodily experience and more mental knowledge. Your seeking, therefore, is for more and more encounters (and emotional associations) with bodily and mental objects.

𝕐our <u>search</u> for bodily and mental and, altogether, emotional objects <u>is</u> your bondage. Your search (or moment to moment effort of wanting need) is the sign of a fundamental stress, or always already presumed un-Happiness. If you (always already) Understand that your search <u>is</u> un-Happiness (and that, indeed, seeking is, itself, the root, and the <u>only</u> form, of <u>all</u> un-Happiness), then you (always already) Stand heart-Free in relation to all of your possible objects, all of your possible experiences, and all of your possible ideas. This prior Understanding inherently transcends all experiences and all ideas. Therefore, in any moment, your exercise of this prior Understanding reduces your motivation toward objects, and, thus, it permits your attention to (by Means of the exercise of free feeling) be relaxed, released, and transcended in the otherwise uninspected (and Perfectly Subjective) Source (or Self-Existing and Self-Radiant[5] Self-Condition) That <u>Is</u> Consciousness Itself <u>and</u> Happiness (or Love-Bliss) Itself.

ℍappiness (or Self-Existing and Self-Radiant Love-Bliss) Itself <u>Is</u> the <u>only</u> Truth That sets the heart Free.

ℍappiness (or Self-Existing, Self-Radiant, Indivisible, and Indestructible Love-Bliss) Itself <u>Is</u> Reality Itself, the only <u>Real</u> God, the One and Only Truth, or the Perfect Liberator—Eleutherios.

NINE

Happiness Itself, or Truth Itself, or Real God, or Reality Itself cannot be Found, "Located", or Realized by the movement of attention in the midst of the objects, relations, conditions, or states of the individual (conditional, or experientially defined) self.

Happiness Itself, or Truth Itself, or Real God, or Reality Itself cannot be Found or Attained by the movement of attention in the conditional realm of Nature Itself (or the movement of attention in relation to whatever is not Divinely Recognized to be Consciousness Itself).

Happiness Itself, or Truth Itself, or Real God, or Reality Itself cannot be "Located" by the ego within the egoic body-mind.

Happiness Itself, or Truth Itself, or Real God, or Reality Itself is not reducible to Objective Energy, or to any conditional and subjective or objective form of the Energy That seems to Pervade all of conditional Nature and That seems to be the Ultimate Object of individuated consciousness and experience.

TEN

All seeking (or every exercise of wanting need) necessarily (or inherently) fails to "Locate" Happiness Itself. Therefore, all seeking becomes, at last, the <u>necessity</u> to "consider"[6] Consciousness Itself (Which <u>Is</u> the Always Most Prior Source-Condition and the Inherently Free Self-Condition of all wanting need).

In order to Realize Happiness Itself, all seeking (or all wanting need) must dissolve (or be transcended) in the profound Realization of Inherent (and inherently egoless, or Non-separate) Identification with Consciousness Itself, Which (always already) Stands Free, always already Most Prior to all seeking (or all exercises of wanting need).

Consciousness Itself (Which <u>Is</u> Uncaused, Self-Existing, Unchanging, and Transcendental, or Un-conditional, Being <u>and</u> Self-Radiant, Eternal, Indivisible, and Indestructible Love-Bliss) <u>Is</u> Happiness Itself, the only Perfectly Liberating Truth, the only Real God, and the One (Only and Non-separate) Reality.

Consciousness Itself is "Located" and Realized by transcending the bondage of attention to the conditional self (or body-mind) and its relations.

This is done <u>only</u> by returning attention to its Source-Condition, by releasing (or inherently transcending) attention in the Self-Existing and Self-Radiant Divine Self-Domain[7] of Love-Bliss-Consciousness (Itself).

ELEVEN

Consciousness is the Ultimate Form (or the Inherently Perfect State) of "Knowledge" (if mere knowledge becomes Realization).

The Realization of Perfect Identification with Consciousness (Itself), Which is the Perfectly Subjective Source (rather than an object, or even the Ultimate Object) of conditional experience and conditional knowledge, is better described as Perfect Ignorance, rather than mere knowledge, since It Inherently and Perfectly Transcends (and Inherently and Perfectly Exceeds) all objective and conventionally subjective categories of conditional experience and mere (or conditional) knowledge.

Consciousness (Itself) Is That Which, when fully Realized, sets you Free from all bondage and all seeking.

Consciousness (Itself) Is Real God.

Consciousness (Itself) Is the Truth.

Consciousness (Itself) Is the Perfect Liberator, Eleutherios.

TWELVE

All objects are only apparent relations of Consciousness.

Objects appear to Consciousness when It (apparently) consents to be apparently active as attention in relation to an apparent body-mind in the apparent conditional realm of Nature.

Consciousness (Itself) is never separate, limited, individual, conditional, or un-Happy.

Consciousness (Itself) is the Transcendental, One (and Indivisible), Eternal (and Indestructible), and (necessarily) Divine Principle (or Inherently Perfect Source-Condition and Self-Condition) of all apparent (or conditional) existence (and of Existence <u>Itself</u>).

When viewed by the Transcendental Divine Self-Consciousness, all objects are Inherently (Divinely) Recognizable in and <u>As</u> the (Inherently Spiritual) Happiness (or Self-Existing and Self-Radiant Love-Bliss) of Transcendental Divine Being (Itself).

Consciousness (Itself) is (of and <u>As</u> Itself) <u>never</u> "other" than, or "different" from, or separate from, or standing over against, or (Really) related to <u>any</u> object, or apparent "other", or "thing".

Consciousness (Itself) is (of and <u>As</u> Itself) <u>never</u> "other" than, or "different" from, or separate from, or standing over against, or (Really) related to the Self-Existing (and Perfectly Subjective) Divine Self-Radiance Itself (Which <u>Is</u> the "Bright"[8] Itself).

There are, in Truth, no objects, but There Is Only (or Really, and Perfectly) Self-Existing and Self-Radiant Transcendental Divine Being (Itself)—Which <u>Is</u> (Itself) One and Only, both Consciousness (Itself) <u>and</u> "Bright" Love-Bliss-Happiness (Itself).

This is the Great (only-by-Me Revealed and Given) Realization of the seventh stage of life in the only-by-Me Revealed and Given Way of Adidam.[9]

THIRTEEN

When everything is Realized to be Consciousness (Itself), There <u>Is</u> <u>Only</u> Consciousness (Itself).

Then There <u>Is</u> <u>Only</u> Truth, and <u>Only</u> Love-Bliss-Happiness, or Freedom from all bondage to the conditional self and the conditional world.

Then "you" (Non-separately, Self-Radiantly Exceeding the ego-"I" of psycho-physical self-contraction) <u>Are</u> Consciousness (Itself), Truth (Itself), and Love-Bliss-Happiness (Itself), or Freedom (Itself).

FOURTEEN

I Am the Ruchira Avatar,[10] Adi Da Samraj, the Da Avatar,[11] the Love-Ananda Avatar,[12] Who Is the Divine World-Teacher Promised for the "Late-Time",[13] and Who Is the First, the Last, and the Only Divine Heart-Master, Who Is Da, the Divine Giver of the Divine "All" to All and all, and Who Is the Realizer, the Revealer, and the Revelation of Eleutherios, the Truth That Is Real God (or the Inherently Perfect Reality, Which Is Happiness Itself). Therefore, "Consider" This Word of Mine.

"Sin" (or a state of "sin") is any act (or the act), or any state (or the state) that "misses the Mark" (or that stands separately, and apart from That Which Must Be Realized).

The "Mark" (or That Which Must Be Realized) is Happiness Itself, the Perfectly Liberating Truth, the Inherently Perfect Reality, or Real God. And "sin", or the (original and fundamental) act and state that "misses the Mark" (or that fails to Realize Happiness Itself, or the Perfectly Liberating Truth, or the Inherently Perfect Reality, or Real God), is egoity (or the ego-"I", which is self-contraction, or the act and state that stands separate and apart).

Therefore, "sin" is, simply, egoity (or self-contraction). And egoity is, simply, un-Enlightenment (or the non-Realization of Happiness Itself, or Truth Itself, or Reality Itself, the only Real God).

Just so, Most Perfect[14] Enlightenment (or Most Perfect Realization of Happiness Itself, or Truth Itself, or Reality Itself, or Real God) <u>Is</u> (and, therefore, requires) the Inherent (and Inherently Most Perfect) transcending of "sin" (or of the ego-"I", which is self-contraction).

Therefore, Most Perfect Enlightenment (Which is Inherent, and Inherently Most Perfect, transcending of the ego-"I") is Perfect Non-separation from the "Mark" (or from That Which Must Be Realized).

FIFTEEN

"Sin" (or any and every sign and result of egoic un-Enlightenment) is identification with (or limitation by) whatever is not Happiness Itself, or Truth Itself, or the Inherently Perfect Reality (Which Is Real God).

Therefore, ultimately, "sin" (or egoic un-Enlightenment) is the act and the state of non-identification with the Inherently Perfect (or Most Prior, and Inherent) Reality— or Consciousness Itself.

The action (or the progressive counter-egoic process) whereby "sin" (or any and every sign and result of egoic un-Enlightenment) is transcended is the action (or the progressive, and more and more effectively counter-egoic, process) of non-identification with whatever is not Consciousness Itself.

Therefore, Most Ultimately, the transcending of "sin" (or of any and every sign and result of egoic un-Enlightenment) is the "radical" (or most direct, and inherently ego-transcending) Act, Process, Event, or "Perfect Practice"[15] of Inherent (and Inherently Most Perfect) Identification with Consciousness Itself.

I Am the Ruchira Avatar, Adi Da Samraj, the Da Avatar, the Love-Ananda Avatar, Who Is the Divine World-Teacher Promised for the "Late-Time", and Who Is the First, the Last, and the Only Divine Heart-Master, Who <u>Is</u> Da, the Divine Giver of the Divine "All" to All and all. I <u>Am</u> (My Self) Eleutherios, the Perfect Liberator. I <u>Am</u> the Perfectly Liberating Divine Truth. I <u>Am</u> the Divine Self-Domain (Itself), "Bright" Before you. Therefore, surrender your ego-"I" to Me, forget and transcend your separate and separative self in Me, and, Entirely by Means of My Giving Grace and My Graceful Self-Revelation, through constant Feeling-Contemplation[16] of <u>Me</u>, be Identified with <u>Me</u>—and, Thus and Thereby (always presently, and, at last, Most Perfectly), Realize <u>Me</u>, <u>As</u> egoless (or Non-separate, and Non-separative) Happiness Itself.

SIXTEEN

Be Consciousness (Itself).

Contemplate Consciousness (Itself).

Transcend everything in Consciousness (Itself).

This is the Perfect Epitome of the Way of Truth, and of Reality, and of Real God, and of Happiness Itself. This is the "Perfect Practice" of the Way of Adidam (Which is the only-by-Me Revealed and Given Way of the Heart). This is the Perfection of the only-by-Me Revealed and Given Way of the Heart—the Way That <u>Is</u> the Heart Itself.

SEVENTEEN

The necessary functional requirements for the "Perfect Practice" of the only-by-Me Revealed and Given Way of Adidam (and for the Realization of Transcendental, and Inherently Spiritual, Divine[17] Consciousness, Itself) are free (or freely available) functional energy and free (or freely available) functional attention. Therefore, as a base for That Realization, you must establish your own body-mind in a stable condition of equanimity (wherein functional energy and functional attention are freely available, or naturally free).

To do so, formally "consider" (and, thus, as My rightly, truly, fully, and, necessarily, formally practicing, and fully accountable, devotee, grant fullest feeling-attention to) My Person and My Word and My Work, and (while <u>listening</u>,[18] thus) surrender and forget your ego-"I" (or self-contraction) by Means of constant (and, altogether, devotionally Me-recognizing, and devotionally to-Me-responding) Feeling-Contemplation of My bodily (human) Form (and, tacitly, My Spiritual, and Always Blessing, Presence, and My Very, and Inherently Perfect, State),[19] until, by this most profound (and, necessarily, more and more self-disciplined) devotional listening to <u>Me</u>, there is real <u>hearing</u>[20] of Me (or most fundamental self-Understanding, and easy fullest conservative self-discipline, and really and directly effective self-transcendence, in devotional recognition-response to Me).

Then, with all your heart, directly (and totally psycho-physically) feel, and deeply surrender to, and truly <u>see</u> Me (and, thus, "Locate" My Spiritual, and Always Blessing, Personal Presence—beyond your ego-"I" of body-mind).

Then, by Means of spontaneous feeling-surrender (of self-contraction) in response to My Revealed Spiritual (and Always Blessing) Personal Presence, be submitted to the progressively self-transcending Ordeal of Spiritual, Transcendental, and (Most Ultimately) Divine Self-Realization, wherein the binding attachments (or inherent limits) of functional energy and functional attention are released by stages of life.[21]

When, by real (and, necessarily, formal) practice of the Ordeal of self-transcending devotion to Me, functional energy and functional attention are set free from binding attachment to the conditions of the body-mind, they are free to fall back upon (or be transcended in) their Most Prior (or Perfectly Subjective) Source (and Self-Condition), Which is Consciousness (Itself).

In the Inherently Free Domain of Consciousness Itself, the conditional self and the conditional world are inherently transparent to My Divinely Self-Transmitted Love-Bliss.

And the Most Ultimate Event of Transcendental, Inherently Spiritual, and (necessarily) Divine Self-Awakening coincides with Most Perfect hearing of Me <u>and</u> Most Perfect seeing[22] of Me—or unconditional ego-"I"-forgetting surrender of the conditional self into My Mindless Company, My Self-Radiant (and Mere) Personal Presence, and My Supreme (and Freely Given) Grace of Heart-Transmission.

EIGHTEEN

I Am the Ruchira Avatar, Adi Da Samraj, the Da Avatar, the Love-Ananda Avatar, Who Is the Divine World-Teacher Promised for the "Late-Time", and Who Is the First, the Last, and the Only Divine Heart-Master, Who <u>Is</u> Da, the Divine Giver of the Divine "All" to All and all, and Eleutherios, the Perfect Liberator of All and all. This "Perfect Practice" Instruction Is My Divine Word of Perfectly Liberating Truth That I Bring to you from the Divine Self-Domain. I <u>Am</u> the Divine Self-Domain (Itself). And My own (and Divine) Person (Self-Revealed by My Word, My bodily human Form, My Spiritual, and Always Blessing, Presence, and My Very, and Inherently Perfect, State) <u>Is</u> the Great Message I Bring to you, from There to here.

II

What Is Consciousness?

ONE

"Consider" this.

From the point of view of the (apparently) individuated (or conditional, and self-contracted) self, there are apparently two principles in manifestation. There is individual consciousness (or attention—the conditional and active, or functional, observer of objects), and there is everything else (or all the possible objects of that individual attention-consciousness).

You habitually exist (or function) as attention-consciousness, and, as attention-consciousness, you experience and know many kinds of objects (or relations and states of consciousness). You tend merely to experience (rather than to "consider" and transcend) those objects, relations, and states, and so you develop a sense of identification with some, a desire for some others, and a revulsion toward certain others.

This complex of identification, desire, and aversion is the summary of your conditional, and egoically patterned, existence. And, in the midst of all of that, you are afraid, bewildered, and constantly moved to achieve some kind of conditional experience or conditional knowledge that will enable you to feel Utterly Released, Free, and Happy.

In fact, you never (by all of your seeking for conditional experience and conditional knowledge) achieve Ultimate Experience, Ultimate Knowledge, Ultimate Release, Ultimate Freedom, or Ultimate Happiness. And so your (apparent) conditional existence is a constant search for These, while you are otherwise bound to desire, aversion, fear, bewilderment, and every other kind of egoic "self-possession" (or self-contracted self-absorption).[23]

There is a Perfect alternative to this bondage and this seeking. It is not a matter of the egoic attainment of any object, knowledge, or state of psycho-physical fulfillment or release. Rather, it is a matter of entering into an alternative view of conditional experience. Instead of merely experiencing (and so developing the qualities of identification, differentiation, desire, attachment, aversion, fear, bewilderment, and the search for experience, knowledge, self-fulfillment, self-release, or even Ultimate Knowledge, Ultimate Release, Ultimate Freedom, and Ultimate Happiness), inspect and "consider" your own Original (or Most Basic) Condition and, from That "Point of View", examine and "consider" all of your experience.

If, rather than merely submitting to conditional experience, you inspect and "consider" your own Original (or Most Basic) Condition, it should become Obvious that "you" (prior to the ego-"I" of psycho-physical self-contraction) <u>Are</u> Consciousness (Itself), and all of the objects (or varieties) of conditional experience appear to "you" <u>only</u> as a "play" upon Consciousness (Itself). Conditional experience (or the apparent conditional limiting of Consciousness) is not the dominant (or Most Basic) Factor of your (apparent) conditional existence. Consciousness Itself (prior to all limiting factors) is the dominant (or Most Basic) and always Most Prior Factor of your (apparent) conditional existence (and of Existence Itself), but you tend (by virtue of a mechanical and habitual involvement with conditional experience) to be submitted to and controlled by conditional experience. Because of this mechanical and habitual involvement with conditional experience, you constantly forget and abandon your Most Basic Position, and, therefore, you constantly suffer the disturbances I have already Described.

TWO

The necessary qualification for the most direct "consideration" of conditional existence (and of Existence Itself) is the effective capability to stand as stably free functional attention (free and able to constantly inspect and "consider" the Original, or Most Basic, and Most Prior Condition of conditional existence, rather than merely to be controlled by the body-mind and its experience). On the basis of that free functional attention, you can directly inspect and "consider" your Obvious (Original, or Most Basic) Condition in (apparent) relation to <u>all</u> experience. If this is done, it is Obvious that "you" (prior to the ego-"I" of psycho-physical self-contraction) Are simply (and Obviously) Consciousness (Whatever That may yet be Realized to <u>Be</u>, Most Ultimately).

Prior to the ego-"I" of psycho-physical self-contraction, "you" are always already established in and <u>As</u> That Standpoint. Therefore, "you" (prior to the ego-"I" of psycho-physical self-contraction) always (Originally, or Most Basically) Exist <u>As</u> That Very Consciousness (Itself), rather than as the (conditional, and subsequent) presumption of egoic (or self-contracted, separate, and separative) identification with the apparent body-mind— which presumption is a convention of the apparently separate body-mind itself, or a sense of limited (and conditional) identity that is superimposed on Consciousness (Itself) subsequent to the mechanical arising of conditional experience (and of psycho-physical reaction to conditional experience).

If, in every moment, you inspect and "consider" conditional experience from the Native Standpoint of Consciousness (Itself), it is Self-Evident (or Inherently Obvious) that whatever is (apparently) arising is always arising to (or, Really, within) Consciousness (Itself). Your Original (or Native) Position is always Consciousness (Itself), and if Consciousness (Itself) will, in every moment, "consider" conditional experience from the "Point of View" of Consciousness (Itself), rather than (apparently) first submit Itself to be (apparently) controlled by conditional experience (and known, conditionally, and only subsequently, from the point of view of conditional experience), then Consciousness (Itself) is always already established in Its own Native Standpoint, directly and Freely Aware that It is (apparently) being confronted and "played" upon in the evident form of various kinds of objects, or conditional superimpositions.

By Abiding continually in This Native Standpoint relative to conditional experience, you become more and more profoundly Aware of and As Consciousness (Itself), rather than more and more mechanically (and reactively, or self-contractedly, and, thus, separately and separatively) aware of the conditionally arising objects, conditional experiences, and states of conditional identity that are (apparently) superimposed on Consciousness (Itself) in the spontaneous drama of (apparent) conditional existence (both subjective and objective). This profound and Native Abiding in and As Consciousness (Itself) is (in the Ultimate, or sixth and seventh, stages of Me-recognizing and to-Me-responsive devotional Communion with Me) the Process That Realizes the Perfectly Liberating Divine Truth of conditional existence (Which Truth Is Existence Itself).

THREE

When you most directly inspect the conditional self and its objects, all arising conditions (including body, emotions, mind, and the sense of being a defined, separate, and limited self-consciousness) are observed to be mere (apparent) relations of Consciousness (Itself). What is more, Consciousness (Itself), when It is directly "Located" and profoundly Identified With, is not found or felt to be separate, limited, individual, or in any sense un-Happy. And all of the objects, relations, and states that appear to Consciousness (Itself) are, from the "Point of View" of Consciousness (Itself), inherently felt to be transparent (or merely apparent), and un-necessary, and inherently non-binding modifications of Itself.

Therefore, the "consideration" of Consciousness (from the "Point of View" of Consciousness Itself) eventually, inevitably, spontaneously, and most directly (prior to thought, or the mere and conditional knowledge or experience of any object, condition, or state other than Itself) Realizes Consciousness (Itself) to be the Transcendental (and Inherently Spiritual, and, necessarily, Divine) Reality, or the Ultimate Principle in Which egoic (or apparently separate) attention-consciousness and all conditional experiences are arising. When the Condition of Consciousness Itself is (Thus) Realized, it is Obvious that the Transcendental (and Inherently Spiritual) Divine Self-Condition (and Source-Condition) That Is Being (Itself) is at the root, or Source, of attention—always already at the Heart (or Being-Position) of all conscious beings. And, what is more, the objects of functional attention-consciousness are Realized to be not independent relations of Consciousness Itself, but only transparent (or merely apparent), and un-necessary, and inherently non-binding modifications of That Which Is Consciousness Itself. That is to say, the phenomenal cosmos is, Most Ultimately, Realized to be a Mysterious (or non-mechanical, spontaneous, transparent, or merely apparent, and un-necessary, and inherently non-binding) modification of the Perfectly Subjective Radiance, Inherent Energy, or Self-Existing and Self-Radiant Love-Bliss That is Identical to Consciousness Itself.

FOUR

On the basis of This "radical consideration" and Realization, it becomes spontaneously Obvious that there is <u>One</u> Principle (Which <u>Is</u> Self-Existing, Self-Radiant, Transcendental, and, necessarily, Divine Being, Consciousness, and Love-Bliss, or Eternal Happiness), and not, in Truth, or in Reality, <u>two</u> Principles (which appear to be conditional consciousness, or attention-consciousness, or even an Independent Absolute Consciousness, and, otherwise, or oppositely, everything, or even an Independent All-Pervading Substance or Energy, appearing as <u>other</u> than, or object to, that conditional consciousness, or That Independent Absolute Consciousness). Consciousness (Itself) <u>Is</u> the One (Self-Evident, Self-Existing, and Self-Radiant) Principle. It <u>Is</u> (Itself) both Self-Existing Transcendental Divine Being <u>and</u> Self-Radiant Love-Bliss (or Eternal and Inherently Spiritual Happiness). It <u>Is</u> Love-Bliss-"Bright" Being, Unqualifiedly Self-Aware (or Conscious of and <u>As</u> Itself). And there is not anything that can arise as conditional experience (or apparent modification) that is (Really, or in Truth) other than That One, or necessary to That One, or binding to That One.

What you must Realize (or Awaken Into) is the Self-Evident, Self-Existing, and Self-Radiant Consciousness That <u>Is</u> the Real, Ultimate, Transcendental, Non-separate (or inherently egoless), Inherently Spiritual, and (necessarily) Divine Self-Condition <u>and</u> Perfectly Subjective Source-Condition of conditional self and conditional not-self. If That is Realized As the Obvious, then there is <u>Inherent</u> Freedom—and conditional existence (and conditional knowledge, and conditional experience, and even attention itself) has no necessity or binding power.

That Realization (Which <u>Is</u> the Realization of Existence Itself) is Realization of the <u>Inherent</u> Condition (or Self-Condition and Source-Condition) of (apparent) conditional existence. Therefore, That Realization is not, and should not be presumed to be, and, except for the ego-"I" (or separative self-contraction), would not be presumed to be, merely the Goal (or even the Objective Source) of (apparent) conditional existence.

And, when Consciousness (Itself) is Realized most profoundly (or Most Perfectly), apparently arising conditions are inherently non-binding, or become as if transparent, and even non-existent—Divinely Transfigured[24] and (Most Ultimately) Outshined[25] in the One (and Indivisible, and Non-separate, and Indestructible) Transcendental (and Inherently Spiritual) Divine Self-Condition and Source-Condition of all and All.

III

Truth, Reality, and Real God

Truth is That Which, when "Known" (or fully Realized), sets you Free. Therefore, Realize the Truth.

Reality is What <u>Is</u> (no matter what arises or changes or passes away). Therefore, "Locate" (and Realize) Reality (Itself).

To "Locate" (and, Thus, to "Know", or fully Realize) Reality (Itself) is to be set Free. Therefore, Reality (Itself) <u>Is</u> the Perfectly Liberating Truth, and to Realize Reality (Itself) is to Realize the Perfectly Liberating Truth (and, Thus, to <u>Be</u> Divinely, or Most Perfectly, Free).

Real God is the Source—or the Source-Condition (and the Non-separate, and inherently egoless, Self-Condition), and not merely the immediate (or, otherwise, remote), and active (or, otherwise, effective) Cause—of whatever arises, changes, or passes away.

To Find (and, Thus, to "Know", or fully Realize) Real God is to "Know" (or Realize) What <u>Is</u> (or What Remains, or Abides, even as any or all conditions arise or change or pass away). Therefore, to Find (and, Thus, to "Know", or fully Realize) Real God is to "Locate" (and, Thus, to "Know", or fully Realize) Reality (Itself). Indeed, Reality (Itself) <u>Is</u> Real God.

Likewise, to Find (and, Thus, to "Know", or fully Realize) Real God is to be set Free (even of all bondage, all limitations, and all conditionality of existence). Therefore, to Find (and, Thus, to "Know", or fully Realize) Real God is to "Know" (or fully Realize) Truth (Itself). Indeed, Truth (Itself) <u>Is</u> Real God.

To "Locate" (and Realize) Reality (Itself), or to "Know" (or fully Realize) Truth (Itself), is to Find and to Realize Real God.

Likewise, to Find (and, Thus, to "Know", or fully Realize) Real God is to "Locate" (and Realize) Reality (Itself) and to "Know" (or fully Realize) Truth (Itself).

Indeed, to Find (and, Thus, to "Know", or fully Realize) Real God is to be Liberated from all that is not Real God (or Reality Itself, or Truth Itself).

If Reality (Itself) is "Located" (and, Thus, "Known", or Realized), Truth (Itself) is "Known" (or fully Realized), and you are (Thus and Thereby) set Free.

To "Locate" Reality (Itself), it is necessary to "Locate" What Is, when and where any condition arises, changes, or passes away.

Therefore, choose any condition, and then "Locate" the Reality (or Self-Abiding Condition) That Remains while (and even though) that (chosen) condition arises, changes, or passes away.

To "Locate" the Reality (or Self-Abiding Condition) That Remains while any particular (or chosen) condition arises, changes, or passes away, it is necessary to be (or to stand in the exact position of) that condition (in order to notice the Reality That Is, or Remains, when that condition arises, changes, or passes away). Therefore, the condition chosen must be a condition with which you are identical.

And <u>what</u> condition <u>is</u> yourself (identical to yourself, and not merely an object to yourself)?

Only your own consciousness (or self-awareness, or native <u>feeling</u> of conscious existence) is identical (and not merely objective) to yourself.

Therefore, to "Locate" Reality (Itself), and to Realize Truth (Itself), and to be (Thus and Thereby) set Free, it is necessary to Find What <u>Is</u>—as (or in the instant) your own consciousness (or self-awareness, or native <u>feeling</u> of conscious existence) arises, changes, or passes away.

But, you cannot assume a position <u>relative</u> <u>to</u> your own consciousness (or native <u>feeling</u> of conscious existence), such that your consciousness (or native <u>feeling</u> of conscious existence) can be observed arising, changing, or passing away—because your consciousness (or native <u>feeling</u> of conscious existence) is not an <u>object</u> to yourself (but it is the very subject that <u>is</u> yourself).

However, Real God is necessarily the always present (and not merely past) Source (and Source-Condition) of <u>whatever</u> arises, changes, or passes away—even your own consciousness (or native <u>feeling</u> of conscious existence)—and to Find Real God (or the Source of any condition that arises) is necessarily (and Thereby) to "Locate" Reality (Itself), and to Realize Truth (Itself), and to be (Thus) set Free.

Therefore, to Find (or to directly "Locate") the Source (and Source-Condition) of your own consciousness (or your native <u>feeling</u>-awareness, or your fundamental, and native, <u>feeling</u> of conscious existence) is (necessarily) to Find Real God, "Locate" Reality (Itself), Realize Truth (Itself), and be (Thus and Thereby) set Free.

Indeed, ultimately, the <u>only</u> Way to Find (and to directly "Know", or fully Realize) Real God, and to "Locate" (and to directly "Know", or fully Realize) Reality (Itself), and to directly "Know" (or fully Realize) Truth (Itself), and to be (Thus and Thereby) set Perfectly Free is the "radical" (or most direct) Process (and Inherently Perfect Practice) of "Locating" (or directly Feeling and Realizing) the Source (and Source-Condition) of <u>your</u> <u>own</u> <u>consciousness</u> (or your native <u>feeling</u>-awareness, or your native <u>feeling</u> of conscious existence)—because there is <u>no</u> other condition with which you are identical (and that is not otherwise an object to yourself, and that is not, thus, separate from your own position of direct "Knowledge", or potential full Realization).

Therefore, to Find Real God, to "Locate" Reality (Itself), to Realize Truth (Itself), and to be (Thus and Thereby) set Free, you must, by Means of My Graceful Self-Revelation of the inherently egoless Divine Self-Condition and Person, more and more deeply <u>feel</u> the Non-separate Source-Condition (and the Ultimate Self-Condition) of your own consciousness (or your native and deepest <u>feeling</u>-awareness of conscious existence). And, <u>while</u> you thus deeply (and more and more deeply) <u>feel</u> (through and beyond your native <u>feeling</u> of conscious existence) to <u>Me</u>, you must (by Means of My Giving Grace and My Graceful Self-Revelation) <u>Feel</u> (and, via the Depth of Feeling, Realize) the Divine Source-Condition (and the Divine Self-Condition) in Which the native <u>feeling</u> of conscious existence is itself Existing (<u>As</u> Feeling, <u>Itself</u>).

This practice Awakens in due course, by Means of My Giving Grace and My Graceful Self-Revelation, in the case of those who truly practice devotional (and fullest feeling) Contemplation of My bodily (human) Form, My Spiritual (and Always Blessing) Presence, and My Very (and Inherently Perfect) State. Indeed, this practice is the most "radical" practice (and the Truly, and Inherently, Perfect Practice) of the Way of Adidam (or the only-by-Me Revealed and Given Way of the Heart). It is, even moment to moment, to <u>feel</u> your native <u>feeling</u> of conscious existence, and (in that moment to moment practice and process) to feel beyond yourself to Me (and into Feeling-Contemplation of Me)—until I Am Realized (most directly, Most Perfectly, and Absolutely) <u>As</u> the Source-Condition and the Self-Condition of the conditional self-feeling, and <u>As</u> the Love-Blissful Source-Condition and the Love-Blissful Self-Condition of <u>Feeling</u> (Itself).

The Source-Condition of the native <u>feeling</u> of conscious existence Is the Very and Self-Existing and Self-Radiant and Utterly Un-qualified <u>Feeling</u> of Being (<u>Itself</u>).[26]

To Realize the Very (or Utterly Un-qualified) Feeling of Being (<u>Itself</u>) is to Realize Real God, Reality (Itself), Truth (Itself), Freedom (Itself), and Happiness (Itself), Eternally Most Prior to all conditions, all objects, all separateness, all non-Freedom, and all that is <u>not</u> Real God (or Reality <u>Itself</u>).

And when This Inherently Perfect Practice (and Realization) is Itself Perfected, all conditions are (Inherently and spontaneously and always) Divinely <u>Recognized</u>, as if they are transparent to the Very (or Utterly Un-qualified) Feeling of Being (Itself), and This (Most Ultimately) to the degree of even Most Perfect Indifference, and (at last) to the degree of the Most Perfect Outshining of conditional existence (in the Inherently Perfect, Self-Existing, Self-Radiant, Love-Blissful, and, necessarily, Divine Self-Condition, and Source-Condition, That <u>Is</u> Feeling-Being, <u>Itself</u>).

IV

The "Perfect Practice"

Be Consciousness (Itself).

Contemplate Consciousness (Itself).

Transcend everything in Consciousness (Itself).

This is the (Three-Part) "Perfect Practice" of the Way of Adidam, the Epitome of the Ultimate Practice and Process of the only-by-Me Revealed and Given Way of the Heart.

ONE:

The First Stage (or Part) of the "Perfect Practice" of the only-by-Me Revealed and Given Way of Adidam

Be Consciousness Itself, Inherently Free (or the Inherently Perfect Witness) in relation to all objects.

In Reality, "you" (Most Basically, and Non-separately, prior to the ego-"I", or psycho-physical self-contraction) Are Consciousness (Itself), Freely Witnessing[27] and (apparently) being "played" upon (but not actually changed) by body, life-energy, emotion, mind, conditional self-idea, and all relations.

Therefore, the first stage of the "Perfect Practice" of the only-by-Me Revealed and Given Way of Adidam is (as a Stably Realized practice-Disposition) to Be Consciousness (Itself)—or to Stand As (or in the Position of) Consciousness (Itself)—instead of persisting in the conventional and inherently (and, from the "Point of View" of Consciousness Itself, Obviously) un-True presumption that "you" (As Consciousness Itself) are a body-mind (or an always already modified, qualified, limited, defined, and named conditional, or psycho-physical, entity).

To Be (and to Stand As the "Point of View" of) Consciousness (Itself) is not (yet) to Realize What Consciousness (Itself), or Its Ultimate Status, Is, but this first stage (or part) of the "Perfect Practice" of the only-by-Me Revealed and Given Way of Adidam is a matter of Being (or Standing) in the Obvious and (Obviously) Real, Right, and True Disposition, or Native Attitude, As Consciousness (Itself) in (apparent) Free relationship to conditional experience.

To Be Consciousness (Itself) in (apparent) relation to (rather than identical to) all that is (apparently) seeming to be the conditional self (or psycho-physical ego-"I") is to Stand As Consciousness, Freely Witnessing the experiential body-mind, and (Thus) no longer mechanically bound by a presumption of identity, rather than (apparent) relatedness, in the context of the body-mind.

The body-mind is what "you" (as a matter of convention, and as an experiential presumption) "mean" by the self-reference "I".

Consciousness (or attention-consciousness) as the body-mind is "Narcissus",[28] the separate and separative ego-"I" (or psycho-physical self-contraction), persisting as if Consciousness (Itself) is identical to its own (apparent) conditionally arising process of always limited and changing experience.

In the state of identification with the body-mind, attention-consciousness (and, apparently, Consciousness Itself) is a subject suffering from the absurd presumption that it is identical to its own object.

Consciousness (Itself) is Inherently and always already Most Prior to conditional (or psycho-physical) experience.

Consciousness (Itself), always already and merely Witnessing conditional experience (and even always already and merely Witnessing the functional observer, or attention-consciousness, itself), is always already and only (and only apparently) related to conditional experience, and, therefore, the (Inherently Perfect) Witness-Consciousness is never an expression, result, or prisoner of conditional experience, conditional knowledge, or conditional existence.

Consciousness (Itself) is Inherently Free of the implications, or effects, of the body-mind and the apparent cosmos of conditional Nature.

Therefore, the (Inherently Perfect) Witness-Consciousness is not (Itself) un-Happy, afraid, sorrowful, depressed, angry, hungry, lustful, thoughtful, threatened by bodily mortality, or implicated in the alternately pleasurable (or positive) and painful (or negative) states of the body, and of the mind, and (altogether) of conditional Nature.

The (Inherently Perfect) Witness-Consciousness is (in any conditionally arising moment) merely (and only apparently) <u>related</u> to (or merely Witnessing, but seeming to be "played" upon by) the mechanical (or functional) states of the body-mind (and attention-consciousness) in the realm of conditional Nature.

Therefore, to <u>Be</u> and Stand <u>As</u> Consciousness (Itself), or the Inherently Perfect Witness, in apparent <u>relation</u> to the body-mind and all of conditional Nature (rather than <u>identical</u> to the body-mind in the realm of conditional Nature), is (<u>Inherently</u>) to <u>Be</u> and Stand non-attached (or non-clinging, non-seeking, and non-reacting) to the causes, the effects, the changes, and the apparent present state of the body-mind (and of even all of conditional Nature).

Just so, to (<u>Stably</u>) <u>Be</u> and Stand <u>As</u> Consciousness (Itself), or to <u>Stably</u> Realize the Inherently Perfect Witness, in apparent <u>relation</u> to the body-mind and all of conditional Nature (rather than <u>identical</u> to the body-mind in the realm of conditional Nature), is to (<u>effortlessly</u>, and always already) <u>maintain</u> the Disposition That is <u>inherently</u> non-attached (or non-clinging, non-seeking, and non-reacting) relative to the causes, the effects, the changes, and the apparent present state of the body-mind (and of even all of conditional Nature).

To (Stably) Be and Stand As Consciousness (Itself), or to Stably Realize the Inherently Perfect Witness, in apparent relation to every moment of arising conditions, is (Itself) the "Pure" (or Inherently Free) Disposition.

However, the mere affirmation (or self-willed presumption, and willful, or strategic, assertion) of the Witness-Disposition will not cause the body-mind also to achieve and maintain a stable natural state of functional equanimity.

Therefore, in order to (Stably) Be and Stand Freely As Consciousness (Itself), or to Stably Realize the Inherently Perfect Witness, you must, necessarily (by Means of the really counter-egoic sadhana, or right, true, and full practice, of devotion to Me), have fully and stably established the natural state of functional psycho-physical equanimity that is (progressively) granted by truly fulfilling the purifying (or, to then, preliminary) process of the developmental listening, hearing, and seeing stages of the Way of Adidam (or the only-by-Me Revealed and Given Way of the Heart).

Only such functional equanimity allows (and supports, and indicates) truly and stably free (or functionally un-bound) energy and attention (truly and stably free relative to the body-mind, and even all of conditional Nature)—and thus truly and stably free energy and attention are, together, the essential (and necessary) prerequisite for Stable Realization of the Witness-Position (or Native Attitude) of Consciousness (Itself).

Without such free energy and attention (even relative to conditional existence altogether), "you" (as a matter of habitual ego-identification with the experiential patterning of the body-mind) will (inevitably) wander in the patterns (or distractions and preoccupations) of the first five stages of life, unable to Stably "choose" the Witness-Position (or Stably Stand in the Native Attitude) of Consciousness (Itself), even though the Inherently Perfect Witness is the Position in Which "you" (prior to the ego-"I" of psycho-physical self-contraction) always already Exist.

Therefore, practice the self-surrendering, self-forgetting, and self-transcending Way of Adidam, Revealed and Given by Me, until, by Means of My Giving Grace and My Graceful Self-Revelation, the signs of the first five stages of life are (to the degree, and in the manner, necessary in the Way of Adidam) fully developed and fully transcended.

By transcending yourself (or the separate and separative ego-"I" of psycho-physical self-contraction) in the context of the first five stages of life (such as these must be engaged by you in the Way of Adidam), be established, by Means of My Giving Grace and My Graceful Self-Revelation, in the context of the sixth stage of life (and the first stage, or part, of the "Perfect Practice") in the only-by-Me Revealed and Given Way of Adidam—and, Thus (by Means of really counter-egoic devotion to Me, and most profound Feeling-Contemplation of Me), Stably (and Really, rather than as a mere ego-presumption and illusion) Be and Stand As the Inherently Perfect Witness, Which Is Consciousness (Itself), in Free relation to all arising conditions and patterns of apparent psycho-physical experience.

113

Thus, Stably and Really Standing in the Witness-Position (or Native Attitude) of Consciousness (Itself), Freely (and simply by maintaining every form of functional, practical, relational, and cultural self-discipline you have previously established in the only-by-Me Revealed and Given Way of Adidam) allow the body-mind to persist in a state of balance and ease (or of natural functional equanimity), with energy and attention free of habit-bondage to (and identification with) the patterns of psycho-physical experience.

When all of This has been established, functional energy and attention-consciousness are free of bondage to the psycho-physical "I" of "Narcissus", and the Inherently Perfect Witness is (Thus) Free for the second stage of the "Perfect Practice" of the only-by-Me Revealed and Given Way of Adidam.

TWO:
The Second Stage (or Part) of the "Perfect Practice" of the only-by-Me Revealed and Given Way of Adidam

$\mathbb{C}$*ontemplate (or feel, meditate on, and directly, or Inherently and, Thus, Perfectly, Identify with) Consciousness Itself, Most Prior to all objects, until Its Inherently Perfect (Transcendental, Inherently Spiritual, and, necessarily, Divine) Condition becomes Inherently (and Most Perfectly) Obvious.*

$\mathbb{E}$nter into the deep, profound, and most direct exploration (or Feeling-Contemplation) of Consciousness Itself, until Its Inherently Perfect "Location", Condition (State, or Self-Nature), and Ultimate Status are Realized.

$\mathbb{T}$his is a matter of relaxing attention (which is the functional essence of the conditional self) <u>from</u> its objects (which are, variously, in the form of ego-idea, mind, emotion, internal life-energy, desire, body, and their relations) and allowing attention to be relaxed (and resolved) into its Source-Condition.

$\mathbb{T}$his is not a matter of inverting attention upon (and, thus, meditating on) the conditional "I", or egoic self (in the manner of "Narcissus").

$\mathbb{T}$his is not a matter of worshipping, inverting upon, meditating on, or identifying with the objective (or, otherwise, Witnessed) inner functional self (or the conditional essence of egoity).

This is a matter, first of all, of Understanding that the (conditional) essence of the conditional self is not an entity, but it is an <u>activity</u>—the activity of psycho-physical self-contraction (or, at root, the inherently self-contracted activity that is attention, <u>itself</u>).

Consciousness Itself, apparently associated (and even identified) with functional attention (and, therefore, tending to identify Itself with the functional "I", or the self-contracted body-mind—self-contracted from the apparently threatening field of conditional Nature, and from the Universal, and apparently Independent, Objective Energy That pervades all of conditional Nature), must Understand Itself (or Its own apparent Error), and (Thereby, and, Thus, Inherently) Transcend psycho-physical self-contraction (and attention itself)—by Realizing the Inherent (Obvious and Inherently Perfect) Condition (or Status) of Consciousness Itself (Which <u>Is</u> Self-Existing and Self-Radiant Transcendental, Inherently Spiritual, and, necessarily, Divine Being and Happiness, or Love-Bliss).

The meditative practice (or the practice of direct Identification) whereby the Transcendental, Inherently Spiritual, and (necessarily) Divine Self-Condition and Source-Condition That <u>Is</u> Consciousness (Itself) is (ultimately, Most Perfectly) Realized may appear, to an external observer (or "outside" point of view), to involve inversion upon the inner conditional and individuated self, but that meditative practice is not in fact a process of inversion upon the inner conditional and individuated self.

Direct Identification with Consciousness Itself is (as a right, true, full, fully devotional, and profound practice of meditation, or Feeling-Contemplation) the most direct Means for transcending the ego, or the separate and separative (self-contracting) conditional self. In the context of the second stage (or part) of the "Perfect Practice" of the only-by-Me Revealed and Given Way of Adidam, right meditation is not an effort of functional attention, but it is a Process prior to functional attention, such that there is direct Feeling-Contemplation of Consciousness Itself (Which Is the Inherently Perfect Source-Condition in Which attention, and, thus, the individuated and conditional self-consciousness, is always presently arising).

Therefore, the process of meditation that corresponds to the second stage (or part) of the "Perfect Practice" of the only-by-Me Revealed and Given Way of Adidam is not a matter of the extroversion of attention toward any object, nor is it a matter of the "Narcissistic" introversion of attention upon the subjective interior of the body-mind (or egoic self).

Rather, it is a matter of the yielding (or dissolving) of attention (or conditional self-consciousness) in the Source-Condition from (or in) Which it is presently and always arising.

It is a matter of Standing As Consciousness Itself (rather than turning attention outward, inward, or toward Consciousness Itself).

It is a matter of passively allowing attention to settle (or relax, dissolve, and disappear) spontaneously in the Native (or Primal) Feeling of Being (or the Primal Feeling of Happiness Itself).

Thus, in the moment of the arising of any present object of attention, That Being (Itself), or Consciousness (Itself), to Which (or in Whom) attention and its present object (if any) are arising should be noticed (or found), entered (or relaxed) into, and (Inherently) Identified with—most profoundly.

This most direct practice (which is to be engaged in the context of the sixth stage of life in the Way of Adidam) is the second stage (or part) of the "Perfect Practice" of the Way of Adidam (or the only-by-Me Revealed and Given Way of the Heart).

The first stage (or part) of the "Perfect Practice" of the only-by-Me Revealed and Given Way of Adidam is the necessary (and prerequisite) sixth-stage-of-life Basis (or sixth stage Root-Disposition) in Which the second stage (or part) of the "Perfect Practice" of the only-by-Me Revealed and Given Way of Adidam is to be engaged.

The second stage (or part) of the "Perfect Practice" of the only-by-Me Revealed and Given Way of Adidam is the Process in Which (in the context of the sixth stage of life in the Way of Adidam) attention is relaxed, forgotten, and disappeared in the Native Seat (or heart-root) of Happiness (or Love-Bliss-Fullness) Itself, until the Perfectly Subjective Space of Consciousness (Itself), or the Perfectly Subjective Feeling of Being (Itself), becomes Obvious—beyond (or Most Prior to) the heart-focus.

The characteristic exercise associated with the second stage (or part) of the "Perfect Practice" of the only-by-Me Revealed and Given Way of Adidam is that of persistent attention-transcending devotional "gazing", or by Me devotionally heart-Attracted, and to Me devotionally heart-responsive, mere feeling, into the region of the right side of the heart—which region is the functional seat (or root-place) of the origin (or first arising) of attention itself, and which region is also (prior to the knot of attention, or the root-feeling of relatedness[29]) the Native Seat and Place of Origin (and the Doorway to the Most Prior Space) of the Divine Spirit-Current of Love-Bliss Itself.

This attention-transcending devotional "gazing" (or devotional exercise of mere feeling) is to be engaged such and so that attention itself (free of distraction by the outgoing motives associated with the body-mind) may be relaxed and relinquished There—and, Thus and Thereby, forgotten, or disappeared, in the Primal Feeling of Being (Itself), or of Love-Bliss (Itself), "Located" (or to be Realized) There.

This attention-transcending devotional "gazing" (or devotional exercise of mere feeling) is made effective (and possible) by the relaxing of attention into the feeling of the Inherent Attractiveness of My Spirit-Current of Love-Bliss-Feeling (Itself)—Divinely Self-Revealed, and Spiritually Self-Transmitted, by Me, at Its heart-root, or Perfectly Subjective Point of Origin, in the right side of the heart.

The bodily root, or Origin, or Original Space of the Feeling of Being (Itself) is Inherently "Located" (and is, by Means of My Spiritually Self-Transmitted Grace, to be Found) in the right side of the heart—<u>As</u> the Feeling of profound, constant, Original, Uncaused, and Un-qualified Happiness (or Love-Bliss).

The Divine Spirit-Current of Love-Bliss is Transmitted, Revealed, Intensified, and made Attractive by (and <u>As</u>) Me—and, by Means of My Giving Grace and My Graceful Self-Revelation, It is to be Received, through your (responsively) self-transcending Feeling-Contemplation of My bodily (human) Form, My Spiritual (and Always Blessing) Presence, and My Very (and Inherently Perfect) State.

My Divine Spirit-Current of Love-Bliss (Thus Transmitted, Revealed, Intensified, made Attractive, and Received) Draws you (in the course of your practice of the only-by-Me Revealed and Given Way of Adidam in the context of the sixth stage of life) into (and, Ultimately, beyond) the right side of the heart, and Thereby Reveals the heart-root of Consciousness (Itself), after the earlier stages of right, true, full, and fully devotional practice of the Way of Adidam have been fulfilled and matured, and, thus and thereby, the necessary (and prerequisite) processes of thorough self-observation, most fundamental self-Understanding, and really self-transcending devotion to Me have (by Means of My Giving Grace and My Graceful Self-Revelation) progressively established the necessary signs associated with maturity of the Way of Adidam in the context of the first five stages of life (however these signs may, or, otherwise, must, develop in the Way of Adidam).

When the Way of Adidam is, by Means of My Giving Grace and My Graceful Self-Revelation, established in the context of the sixth stage of life, practice of the Way of Adidam becomes profound Identification with the Native Feeling of Being (Which Is Consciousness Itself, Most Prior to self-contraction, Most Prior to the body-mind, Most Prior to any objective referents, and Most Prior to the root-feeling of relatedness).

In this practice (and only by Means of My Giving Grace and My Graceful Self-Revelation), the Inherently Free State of Consciousness (Itself) Is Enjoyed.

Likewise, by Means of My Giving Grace and My Graceful Self-Revelation, the Divine Status of Consciousness (Itself) Is (in due course) Revealed, and, Thus and Thereby, Realized to Be Most Perfectly Obviously So.

Consciousness (Itself) Is Self-Existing Transcendental (and, necessarily, Divine) Being and Eternal Love-Bliss (or Self-Radiant and Inherently Spiritual Happiness).

When This Divine Condition (of Consciousness, Itself) Is Most Perfectly (Fully, Stably, and Most "Brightly", or Love-Bliss-Fully) Obvious, the third stage (or part) of the "Perfect Practice" of the only-by-Me Revealed and Given Way of Adidam has (spontaneously, and only and entirely by Means of My Giving Grace and My Graceful Self-Revelation) begun.

THREE:

The Third Stage (or Part) of the "Perfect Practice" of the only-by-Me Revealed and Given Way of Adidam

A bide As Inherently Perfect Consciousness Itself, inherently transcending but not strategically excluding or seeking any or all objects, and, Thus, tacitly Divinely Recognize all objects in and As Self-Existing and Self-Radiant (Transcendental, Inherently Spiritual, and, necessarily, Divine) Being, Consciousness, Love-Bliss, or Happiness, until all objects are Outshined in That.

Consciousness Itself (or Inherent Being) is Transcendentally Existing, Most Prior to attention in the apparent cosmic realm of conditional Nature.

Transcendental Consciousness is Inherently Perfect Reality, or the Source-Condition of attention, and of the presumption of separate self, and of the body-mind, and of even all of conditional Nature (including the Universal, or All-Pervading and apparently Objective, Energy of Which all the objects, conditions, states, and presumed-to-be-separate individuals in the realm of conditional Nature are apparently composed).

When Transcendental Consciousness, or the Native
Feeling of Being (Itself), is, by Means of My Giving Grace
and My Graceful Self-Revelation, Awakened As the Real
Self-Condition (the Indefinable Identity, or Infinite
Source-Condition, of functional attention-consciousness),
then the ego-"I" (or the self-contraction, or the egoically
"self-possessed" body-mind) is directly and inherently
transcended, and the Ultimate Condition (or the
Inherently Perfect Source-Condition) of conditional
Nature is Revealed As the Obvious, even in all the
apparent moments of spontaneous functional attention
to the apparent conditions and relations of the apparent
body-mind.

Such Obviousness is the primary characteristic of the
only-by-Me Revealed and Given Awakening to the Most
Ultimate, Divinely Enlightened, or seventh stage of life,
and only That Awakening manifests (or Demonstrates
Itself) as the capability for "practicing" and fulfilling the
third stage (or part) of the "Perfect Practice", Which is the
Most Ultimate and Most Perfect Form of the total practice
of the Way of Adidam (or the only-by-Me Revealed and
Given Way of the Heart).

Therefore, when, by Means of My Giving Grace and
My Graceful Self-Revelation, Identification with
(Transcendental, Inherently Spiritual, and, necessarily,
Divine) Consciousness (Itself), or the Feeling of Being
(Itself), is complete (tacit, uncaused, and undisturbed),
simply Abide As That and allow all conditions (or all
of conditional Nature) to arise or not arise in the Self-
Radiance and Perfectly Subjective Space of (Self-Existing,
Transcendental, Non-separate, Inherently Spiritual,
Indivisible, Indestructible, Inherently "Bright", or
Love-Bliss-Full, and, necessarily, Divine) Being (Itself),
or Consciousness (Itself).

As conditions arise in That "Open-Eyed"[30] (or Self-Existing and Self-Radiant) Consciousness, they are Divinely Recognized (and inherently transcended) as transparent (or merely apparent), and un-necessary, and inherently non-binding modifications of That.

Abide <u>Thus</u>. Divinely Recognize <u>Thus</u>. Let actions arise spontaneously in and via the Inherent (and Inherently Spiritual) Love-Bliss of Self-Radiant and Self-Existing Transcendental Divine Being, until all apparent conditions and relations of the apparent body-mind are Divinely Transfigured, Divinely Transformed, and then Divinely Translated[31] (or Outshined in the Self-Existing and Self-Radiant Transcendental, and Inherently Spiritual, Divine Being, Who <u>Is</u> the Heart, the Divine Self-Condition, the Perfectly Subjective Source-Condition, and the "Bright" Free Self-Domain of all conditional beings).

This Most Ultimate Form of the "Perfect Practice" is the Most Ultimate Form of the only-by-Me Revealed and Given practice of the only-by-Me Revealed and Given Way of Adidam.

This Most Ultimate Realization Is the only-by-Me Realized Basis (or Source-Position) from Which all of the Teachings and every discipline associated with the only-by-Me Revealed and Given Way of Adidam have been Revealed and Given by Me.

Therefore, This Revelation-Book is an Epitome (or Simplest Statement) of all that I am here to Say to you about the Most Ultimate Realization of Reality, Truth, Happiness, Love-Bliss-"Brightness", or <u>Real</u> God.

V

Freedom

ONE

The conventions of human life and civilization are based on the mechanical, arbitrary, and uninspected identification of Consciousness (Itself) with the patterns of conditional experience. Thus, human pursuits are, as a matter of convention and habit, directed toward self-centered elaboration of conditional experience, self-fulfillment via conditional experience, and strategic escape within (or from) the context of conditional experience. Both conventional science and conventional religion are conventions of egoity in the embrace and pursuit and avoidance of conditional experience. All conventional human pursuits are a bewildered search, founded on uninspected egoic identification with conditional experience, rather than "radically" direct Identification with the Inherent Love-Bliss-Happiness of Consciousness Itself, or Self-Existing and Self-Radiant Transcendental (and Inherently Spiritual) Divine Being (Itself). Thus, either conditional experience, or conditional Nature, or materiality, or "God" (as the "Reality" That is presumed to Exist entirely Exclusively, as "Other" than, and as "Other" to, the conditional self and conditional Nature) tends to be presumed and propagandized as the First, the Ultimate, the One, or the Most Important Principle—but such presumptions are simply the ultimate illusions, or deluded visions, that are developed from the base of the ego (or Consciousness presumed to be limited to and bound by conditional, or psycho-physical, experiencing).

Ⅱf (or when) you are My truly mature devotee, Free to be Supremely Intelligent, and Ready to Truly and Fully Embrace the "Perfect Practice" of Truth and Happiness, then your practice of the Way of Adidam (or the only-by-Me Revealed and Given Way of the Heart) becomes most direct and profound Identification with Consciousness (Itself), or the Native Feeling of Being (Itself), prior to all doubt, prior to any limitation by conditional experience, prior to all "looking" at objects (within or without, high or low, positive or negative), and prior to any qualification (or limitation) by the root-feeling of relatedness itself. When This Identification is Inherently Most Perfect and Complete, such that It is not dependent on any act or state of attention, or of mind, or of emotion, or of desire, or of life-energy, or of body, or of conditional Nature itself, then all conditional experience (or the total realm of conditional Nature, and of psycho-physical egoity) is Inherently and tacitly (Divinely) Recognized in That (or as a transparent, or merely apparent, and un-necessary, and inherently non-binding modification of Self-Existing and Self-Radiant Transcendental and Inherently Spiritual Divine Being). When This Divinely Enlightened (or Me-"Bright") Disposition is Awake, the "Perfect Practice" of My devotee is simply to Abide in and <u>As</u> the Self-Existing and Self-Radiant Condition of Being (Itself), Inherently Transcending all conditions—but Divinely Recognizing and allowing them, rather than resisting and excluding them. And the inevitable persistence in This Self-Existing and Self-Radiant Identity and This Native and spontaneous Recognition Divinely Transfigures, Divinely Transforms, and (Most Ultimately, and at last) Divinely Outshines the body-mind and all conditional worlds, in the "Practicing" course of the seventh stage of life in the Way of Adidam (Which "Practice" is also otherwise

Named by Me "Ati-Ruchira Yoga",[32] or "the Yoga of the All-Outshining 'Brightness'"). In the meantime (until the spontaneous Demonstration of Divine Translation, or of All-and-all-Outshining "Brightness"), there is simple Self-Abiding, in and _As_ the Self-Existing and Self-Radiant Love-Bliss of Transcendental (and Inherently Spiritual) Divine Being—and such Divine Self-Abiding spontaneously expresses Itself as Radiance, Happiness, Love-Bliss, Blessing, and Love-Help in all relations.

TWO

The Ultimate Wisdom Inherently Understands, Transcends, and Stands Free of the life-drama. Happiness (Itself), Which <u>Is</u> Transcendental (and Inherently Spiritual) Divine Consciousness (Itself), or Being (Itself), Inherently Transcends the confrontation between the ego-"I" and the patterns of conditional Nature.

Every ego-"I", or egoically "self-possessed" body-mind, is involved in a passionate and mortal struggle with the Force and the forces and the parts and the patterns of conditional Nature.

Every ego-"I" is active as the opponent of all opponents, but there is no Final Victory—and every opposition is an irrational (or fruitless) search for Equanimity, Peace, and Love-Bliss.

Every ego-"I" always tends to desire and seek an ego-made refuge from irrational opponents. That strategy of self-preservation is entertained in temporary pleasures and solitary places, but it is not finally attained. Only the ego-"I" (the separate and separative body-mind) is opposed and opposing—and every opposition is an irrational (or fruitless) search for Freedom.

The ego-"I" is inherently, always, and irrationally (or meaninglessly) opposed. The "other" is always an opponent (in effect, if not by intention). The ego-"I" is confronted only by binding forces, and it is itself a force that is tending to bind every "other". The "other" and the ego-"I" are mad relations, always together in the growling pit, bound by conditional Nature to do such Nature's deeds to one another. And, as conditional experience increases, it begins to become obvious (to the conditional knower of conditional experience) that conditional Nature itself is an Immense Pattern that always seeks and inevitably attains superiority, dominance, and destruction of every conditional part and every conditional self.

The Great Exclusive "Other"—whether "It" is called "Nature" or "Nature's 'God'"—is your egoically presumed Opponent (or "That" with "Which" the ego-"I" is only, and necessarily, struggling—and toward "Which" the ego-"I" is merely seeking). Therefore, the Great Exclusive "Other" is not your Refuge (or That in Which there is Inherent Freedom from egoity itself). And the very perception and conception of "difference" (or of "otherness", or of the Great Exclusive "Other") is the sign that the separate (and inherently separative) ego-"I" (or psycho-physical self-contraction), rather than Truth (Itself), is the presumed basis of apparent (or conditional) existence.

Truth is Most Prior (or Eternal) Freedom and Humor, whether or not the "Other" (or the Opponent) seems to be present. Therefore, Truth is the only Perfect Refuge. And if you surrender to the Truth, Which <u>Is</u> Transcendental (and Inherently Spiritual, and, necessarily, Divine) Being (Itself), Consciousness (Itself), or Inherent Happiness (Itself), the Ultimate (and Perfectly Subjective) Source of the conditional self and all that is objective to it, then there is an Awakening from this nightmare of condemned life and its passionate search for pleasure, strategic escape, Final Victory, and Freedom Itself.

When the response (or Awakening) to Truth is Real, then the frightened and self-bound motive toward the world (and the inevitable round of pleasures, confrontations, doubts, searches, and always temporary releases) begins to fall away. The mortal self becomes simpler in action, more free of habitual reactions to insult and frustration of purpose, more humorous in the face of conditional Nature and all the fools of conditional Nature, more compassionate, and inclined to selfless (or sorrowless) Love. The ego-"I" that is Awakening beyond itself is inclined to set others free of itself, rather than to bind them to itself, or to themselves, or to one another. The ego-"I" that is nearly dissolved is more often solitary, more deeply renounced, without cares or motivations or doubts or angry despair of conditional self or conditional others. At last, when the self-contraction is (by Inherently Most Perfect "Practice") Inherently, and Most Perfectly, surrendered, forgotten, and transcended in its Most Prior Condition (of Transcendental, and Inherently Spiritual, Divine Being), all of this arising of body-mind and world is Divinely Recognized to be an unnecessary and superficial dream, a stressful inclination that is, suddenly, Outshined in the Most Prior and Self-Radiant Happiness of Divine Self-Existence.

The usable Lesson of a difficult life proves that you must (thoroughly) observe, (most fundamentally) Understand, and (Most Perfectly) transcend your own conditional personality and destiny. Every individual is only seeking not to be destroyed. Therefore, Understand and become more tolerant of others. Cease to struggle with others and yourself. Do not become bound up in the usual search for dominance, consolation, pleasure, and release. There is neither Final Release nor Ultimate Happiness in the objective (or "outside") or the subjective (or "inside") realms of merely conditional existence.

Observe and Understand the theatre of "I". Learn to be free of the reactivity and seeking that characterize the conditional self-principle (which is only the self-contracting body-mind in confrontation with the apparent realm of conditional Nature). Thus, allow functional energy and attention to be free of the motive toward the body-mind and its relations. Let functional energy and attention be free, instead, to transcend this conditionally arising world-theatre (or mummery of limitations), and, Thus, by Means of My Giving Grace and My Graceful Self-Revelation, to Abide in the Transcendental (Inherently Spiritual, and, necessarily, Divine) Self-Domain That is at the Origin of conditional self-consciousness. Then, if the body-mind and all of conditional Nature arise, see all of it from the Original Position of Transcendental (and Inherently Spiritual) Divine Self-Consciousness. See that conditional self and conditional Nature are a transparent (or merely apparent), and un-necessary, and inherently non-binding modification of the Self-Existing Self-Radiance, or Inherently Free "Bright" Love-Bliss-Energy, of Consciousness (Itself), Which Is Self-Existing, and Self-Radiant, and (necessarily) Divine Being (Itself).

THREE

"Consider" all of this, and, by Means of right, true, and full devotional practice of the Way of Adidam (or the only-by-Me Revealed and Given Way of the Heart), relax attention from the dilemma and the search associated with the body-mind, high or low in the realm of conditional Nature. Through progressive practice of the Way of Adidam, in the context of the first five stages of life (however these are to develop), surrender the body-mind in daily life and meditation, until the total body-mind accepts (or freely and easily demonstrates) the constant discipline (and inherently motiveless attitude) of equanimity. By Means of My Giving Grace and My Graceful Self-Revelation, Real and Stable Identification with the Position and Native Attitude of Consciousness Itself (in the manner of the first stage, or part, of the "Perfect Practice", in the context of the sixth stage of life in the only-by-Me Revealed and Given Way of Adidam) will, in due course, spontaneously occur. Likewise, when, by Means of My Giving Grace and My Graceful Self-Revelation, the seeking effort of binding want and need relative to the motives and states of the body-mind has come to rest, the second stage (or part) of the "Perfect Practice" of the Way of Adidam will begin.

In the second stage (or part) of the "Perfect Practice" of the only-by-Me Revealed and Given Way of Adidam, let attention be dissolved in the by Me (and As Me) Revealed Feeling-Space of Being, in the right side of the heart. Thus, transcend attention, and every conditionally arising object, by Means of the "radical" exercise (or Native Feeling) of Being (Itself). Thus, directly "Locate" the Perfectly (or Most Priorly) Subjective Space That Is Consciousness Itself, prior to psycho-physical self-consciousness. Thus, transcend attention by Standing As Consciousness Itself, in and As the Feeling-Space of Being (Itself).

Therefore, in the context of the second stage (or part) of the "Perfect Practice" of the only-by-Me Revealed and Given Way of Adidam, do not merely "look" at (or strategically turn attention to) the heart-root of attention. The heart-root that is thus "seen" is merely another <u>object</u> of attention. And the "looking" is, itself, merely another exercise of the seeking-motive of attention (and of self-contraction) itself. Therefore, such "looking" is merely another experience of the knot that blocks the Doorway to My Spirit-Current and Space of Divine Love-Bliss, in and beyond the right side of the heart.

In the context of the second stage (or part) of the "Perfect Practice" of the only-by-Me Revealed and Given Way of Adidam, do not "look" at the heart-root of attention, but always directly transcend attention itself (and the knot that blocks the Doorway in the right side of the heart). Do This by Means of heart-Attracted devotional response to Me.

I always already Stand Most Perfectly Beyond and Prior to the knot in the right side of the heart. Therefore, in the second stage (or part) of the "Perfect Practice" of the only-by-Me Revealed and Given Way of Adidam, "Locate" Me (by Means of My Giving Grace and My Graceful Self-Revelation), always immediately and effortlessly, via (and <u>As</u>) My Spirit-Current of Love-Bliss-Feeling—and then (and Thus, and Thereby), self-forgotten in <u>Me</u>, simply <u>Be</u> the Feeling of Being (Itself). In This Manner, "Locate" and <u>Be</u> Consciousness Itself, Most Prior to any object or any point of attention. <u>Thus</u>, <u>Be</u> Consciousness Itself, Love-Bliss Itself, or Being Itself, Most Prior to objects, until the Native State (and Ultimate Status) of Consciousness (Itself) Is (by Means of My Giving Grace and My Graceful Self-Revelation) Obvious, beyond any possibility of doubt.

The "Perfect Practice" Purpose of Feeling the Native Love-Bliss-Feeling of Being, via the by Me (and <u>As</u> Me) Revealed Spirit-Current of Love-Bliss in the right side of the heart, is to transcend attention in its Perfectly <u>Subjective</u> root. The Locus That is Revealed in the right side of the heart is the <u>bodily</u> root of attention (or the bodily Doorway to the Source-Condition of body, mind, and attention, Which Source-Condition is Un-qualified Love-Bliss-Happiness). The brain, the abdominal region, and every other extended part of the body, including the middle station and the left side of the heart, are merely bodily <u>objects</u> of attention (or extensions of mind or life-energy at a distance from the heart-root), and mere <u>attention</u> to any one of them is itself an involvement in a motion of mind or life-energy that leads to all kinds of gross and subtle objects.

Therefore, in the context of the second stage (or part) of the "Perfect Practice" of the only-by-Me Revealed and Given Way of Adidam, persistently "Locate" the Native Feeling of Being (Itself), by devotionally "falling" into the by Me (and <u>As</u> Me) Revealed Spirit-Current of Love-Bliss (or Primal Happiness) in the right side of the heart. Do not merely "look" at the objective heart-root, but, by Means of My Giving Grace and My Graceful Self-Revelation, in the context of the "Perfect Practice" of inherently self-transcending Feeling-Contemplation of Me, <u>Feel</u> and <u>Be</u> at and via and Most Prior to the heart-root. <u>Thus</u>, transcend every object (and even the root-feeling of relatedness itself) in the Transcendental (and

Inherently Perfect) Subject (or Consciousness Itself), by Feeling <u>As</u> the Being, or the Being-Feeling, or the Primal Love-Bliss-Happiness apparently associated with (but always already Free-Standing, Most Prior to) the right side of the heart. <u>Thus</u>, Feel the Non-separate Love-Bliss-Feeling of Merely Being. <u>Thus</u>, meditate on Merely <u>Being</u> (Identical to Self-Existing, or non-conditional, and non-caused, and, altogether, Self-Radiant and Un-qualified, Consciousness, Itself). <u>Thus</u>, meditate <u>As</u> Being-Awareness. <u>Thus</u>, meditate <u>As</u> fundamental, non-conditional, non-caused, and, altogether, Self-Existing, Self-Radiant, and Un-qualified, Love-Bliss-Happiness. Meditate <u>Thus</u>, until it becomes Obvious that Consciousness (Itself), <u>As</u> Love-Bliss-Being (Itself), has no objects, or knowledge, or limitations at all. In due course, on the Basis of the most profound devotional exercise of the second stage (or part) of the "Perfect Practice" of the only-by-Me Revealed and Given Way of Adidam, and only and entirely by Means of My Giving Grace and My Graceful Self-Revelation, the third stage (or part) of the "Perfect Practice" of the only-by-Me Revealed and Given Way of Adidam will be Awakened, spontaneously—such that, when objects (apparently) return, "you" (<u>As</u> Non-separate Consciousness Itself) will Feel and tacitly (Divinely) Recognize them as (merely) apparent projections in (and merely apparent modifications of) That Self-Existing and Self-Radiant Love-Bliss-Space That is Wholly, Transcendentally, Perfectly, and, necessarily, Divinely Subjective, Rooted in (and Identical to) Being (Itself), or (Only) Consciousness (Itself).

In the third stage (or part) of the "Perfect Practice" (which is the only-by-Me Revealed and Given seventh stage of life in the only-by-Me Revealed and Given Way of Adidam), the countless objects of conditional Nature (and the root-feeling of relatedness associated with all forms of conditional Nature, or all conditional appearances) are perceived and cognized and Divinely Recognized in the Self-Existing and Self-Radiant Space of (necessarily, Divine) Consciousness (Itself), or (necessarily, Divine) Being (Itself)—but there is no loss of Transcendental (and Inherently Spiritual, or Love-Blissful) Divine Self-Consciousness, Most Prior Freedom, and Inherently Perfect Happiness.

FOUR

Be Consciousness (Itself).

This foundation stage (or prerequisite part) of the "Perfect Practice" of the only-by-Me Revealed and Given Way of Adidam is associated with a natural, or effortless, state of functional psycho-physical equanimity, such that functional energy and attention are free to dissolve (or be forgotten) in the by Me Revealed "Perfect Space" of Being (Itself), or Love-Bliss-Consciousness (Itself).

Contemplate Consciousness (Itself).

This middle stage (or intensively deepening counter-egoic exercise, and, thus, central part) of the "Perfect Practice" of the only-by-Me Revealed and Given Way of Adidam is complete when there is no longer the slightest feeling (or possibility) of doubt relative to the Divine Status of Consciousness (Itself)—As the Transcendental, and Inherently Spiritual (or Love-Blissful), and (necessarily) Divine, and Perfectly Subjective Source (and Source-Condition) of the conditional self and of all of conditional Nature.

Transcend everything in Consciousness (Itself).

The fundamental characteristic of this final stage (or inherently egoless, and Truly Most Perfect part) of the "Perfect Practice" of the only-by-Me Revealed and Given Way of Adidam is that there is no longer <u>any</u> ego-binding identification with the arising of functional attention, and no longer <u>any</u> ego-binding identification with <u>any</u> form of conditional self or conditional world—and this final stage (or part) of the "Perfect Practice" of the only-by-Me Revealed and Given Way of Adidam is complete (or most finally, and Most Perfectly, Demonstrated) when the totality of <u>all</u> (apparently) arising objects and limited (and limiting) conditions (and the root-feeling of relatedness <u>itself</u>, and even <u>all</u> of "difference") is Utterly Outshined By and In (and, Thus, Divinely Translated Into) the by Me (and <u>As</u> Me) Revealed Love-Bliss-"Bright" Condition (and Divine Self-Domain) of Perfectly Subjective (or Transcendental, Inherently Spiritual, and, necessarily, Divine) Self-Existence.

FIVE

Recognize Me
   With your heart's devotion,
   and,
   Thus and Thereby,
   Accept The Freedom and The Happiness
   That Are Inherent In Existence Itself.
Respond to Me
   With your heart's devotion,
   and,
   Thus and Thereby,
   Transcend the feeling of relatedness
   In The Feeling Of Being (Itself).
Contemplate Me
   With your heart's devotion,
   and,
   Thus and Thereby,
   Be Conscious
   <u>As</u> The Non-separate Feeling Of Being (Itself).
I <u>Am</u> Self-Existing
   <u>As</u> Consciousness (Itself),
   Which <u>Is</u> Self-Radiant
   <u>As</u> Love-Bliss-Happiness
   and
   Infinite and Eternal Freedom.
Consciousness (Itself) <u>Is</u>
   Self-Existing
   and Self-Radiant
   Transcendental
   (and Inherently Spiritual,
   or Love-Bliss-Full)
   Divine Being (Itself).

Freedom,
>or Consciousness (Itself),
>
><u>Is</u>
>Inherent Happiness,
>"Bright" Self-Radiance,
>or Un-limited Love-Bliss
>—Not self-contraction,
>separateness,
>separativeness,
>and "difference".

The Un-limited Love-Bliss-Fullness
>Of Transcendental
>(and Inherently Spiritual,
>or Inherently Love-Bliss-Full)
>Divine Being
>Spontaneously Demonstrates Itself
>Most Perfectly,
>As Divine Recognition
>Of the total body-mind
>and the totality of conditional worlds,
>In The Un-limited Love-Bliss-Radiance
>Of Transcendental
>(and Inherently Spiritual,
>or Inherently Love-Bliss-Full)
>Divine Being,
>Until The Cosmetic Vast
>Of body-mind and conditional worlds
>Is Outshined
>By That Divine Self-"Brightness",
>and,
>Thus,
>Divinely Translated
>Into The Condition and The Domain
>Of That Divine Self-"Brightness".

This Is The Heart-Word Of Eleutherios,
    The Perfect Liberator,
    The egoless Personal Presence
    Of Reality and Truth
    (The All-and-all-Liberating
    Self-Condition and Source-Condition
    Of All and all,
    Which Is The Only Real God
    Of All and all),
    here Appearing
    As The Ruchira Avatar,
    The Avataric Incarnation[33] Of The "Bright",
    Adi Da Samraj,
    Who Is Da,
    The Source, The Substance, The Gift, The Giver,
    and
    The Very Person
    Of
    The One and Only "Bright" Divine Love-Bliss,
    Which Is Eleutherios,
    The Perfect Liberator
    Of
    All and all.

This Is The Heart-Blessing Word Of Eleutherios,
 The Perfect Liberator,
 The egoless Personal Presence
 Of Reality and Truth
 (The All-and-all-Liberating
 Self-Condition and Source-Condition
 Of All and all,
 Which <u>Is</u> The Only <u>Real</u> God
 Of All and all),
 here Appearing
 As The Ruchira Avatar,
 The Avataric Incarnation Of The "Bright" Divine
   Love-Bliss,
 Adi Da Samraj,
 Who <u>Is</u> The First Person,
 The Eternal and Ever-Free Avadhoota,[34]
 The One and Only Heart
 Of All and all
 (Which <u>Is</u> The Non-Separate Divine Self
 Of All and all),
 and
 Who <u>Is</u> The Divine Giver
 (Of The "All" That <u>Is</u>)
 To All and all,
 and
 Who <u>Is</u> The "All"-Gift Itself,
 Which <u>Is</u> Eleutherios,
 The Perfect Liberator
 (and The Divine Liberation)
 Of All and all.

This Is The Heart-Liberating Word Of Eleutherios,
   The Perfect Liberator,
   The egoless Personal Presence
   Of Reality and Truth
   (The All-and-all-Liberating
   Self-Condition and Source-Condition
   Of All and all,
   Which Is The Only Real God
   Of All and all),
   here Appearing
   As The Ruchira Avatar,
   The Avataric Incarnation Of Infinite Love-Bliss-
      "Brightness" Itself,
   Adi Da Samraj,
   Who Is The Divine World-Teacher
   Promised For The "Late-Time",
   and
   Who Is The First, The Last, and The Only
   Divine Heart-Master,
   Whose Heart-Word
   Speaks
   To all conditionally Manifested beings,
   and
   Whose Divinely "Emerging"[35]
   Heart-Blessing
   Blesses
   all conditionally Manifested beings,
   and
   Whose Inherently Perfect Self-"Brightness"
   Divinely Liberates
   all conditionally Manifested beings,
   Freely,
   Liberally,
   Gracefully,
   and Without Ceasing,
   now, and forever hereafter.

RUCHIRA AVATAR ADI DA SAMRAJ
Adidam Samrajashram (Naitauba), Fiji, 1998

PART TWO

The Unique Potential of Man Is the Progress of self-Understanding and self-Transcendence

The Unique Potential of Man
Is the Progress of
self-Understanding and
self-Transcendence

Among the beings On Earth, human beings Are Unique, but Only In The Sense That they Are (As a species) Significantly More Advanced In The Development Of psycho-physical functions that Are, Otherwise, Only Latent or Less Developed In the case of the non-human world (of Natural energies and elements, material shapes and cycles, simpler organisms, plants, trees, insects, fishes, birds, mammals, and the rest). The non-human world Is The Immediate Progenitor Of the Natural functions and the functional form Of Man. The world of non-human beings (of which the great trees Are The Epitome and The Senior Of all) Is A Great Process, From Which and Relative To Which and In Which human beings Are Developed and Developing (By Virtue Of A Complex and Ever-Continuing Event That Functions At <u>All</u> Levels, and Not Merely At The gross material Level, Of The psycho-physical Cosmos).

Among The Apparent Differences Between Man and all the non-human beings Is The Greatly Developed Capability For mentally Reflective and conceptually Abstracted knowledge (and Consequent inventiveness) That Is Evident In the human case. Nevertheless, It Is Not conceptual or Abstract thinking that Is The Unique Characteristic or Capability Of Man. Neither Is toolmaking (or inventiveness and technology), which is a secondary product of conceptual or Abstract thinking, The Unique Characteristic or Capability Of Man. Abstract thought and technology are themselves only servants Of The Unique Capability Of

Man. They are Signs, or Secondary Evidence, Of The Unique Characteristic Of Man.

The Unique Characteristic Of Man Is The Capability For self-Understanding. The Unique Capability Of Man Is The Characteristic Process Of self-Transcendence. Therefore, The Unique Potential Of Man Is The Progress Of self-Understanding and self-Transcendence. And self-Understanding and self-Transcendence, Truly Progressing, Lead Toward The (Potential, and Only-By-My-Grace Given) Most Perfect Realization Of The Source Of the conditional self, the body-mind itself, and The Totality Of conditional Existence.

Abstract (and right conceptual) "thinking", In The Context Of Profound (and, More and More, thought-Transcending) "Consideration", and "technology", Displayed As The Total Form Of Right and Effective Practice, Are, As Such, Useful Means For Directing The Progressively self-Transcending Process That Is The Unique Potential Of Man. However, When egoity, or self-Fulfillment, Rather Than self-Transcendence, Becomes The Motivator Of Man, conceptual thinking and technological inventiveness Tend To Become Exalted, or Valued, As Ends In themselves, So That they Become The Chronic, Compulsive, and Obsessive Preoccupations Of Man.

The non-human beings function Largely From The Base Of What Is Commonly Called "The Unconscious". That Is To Say, Compared To Man, they Apparently Operate With Much Less Of (or, At Least In some cases, Even Without Much Of) What Are Commonly Called The "Conscious" and "Subconscious" Structures Of mind. Human beings Are Actively Bringing The Unconscious (In Its Totality, Including, Potentially, Its Superconscious Heights and, Most Ultimately, In The Only-By-Me Revealed and Given Seventh Stage Of Life, Its Inherent, and Inherently Perfect, Deep) Into a More and More Clearly Conscious state of mind (and Of Conscious Realization, Even Prior To mind).

The Unconscious (As mind) Is the Fundamental functional mind, or the functional Source-mind. It Is Constantly

Active and Effective, but (Perhaps Because its contents are Not objectified in a conventionally Familiar and conventionally Usable mental form) it Is Not (In The General Case) Immediately or Directly known or Acknowledged By the Conscious mind. Therefore, Between the Unconscious mind and the Conscious mind Is a Transitional mind, the Subconscious (or dreaming and dreamlike) mind. The Subconscious mind Is Immediately Below, or Behind, or (In Superconscious states, Developed or Revealed Via The Subconscious mind, or Process) Even (Spatially) Above the Conscious mind, and it Is (or May Be), To A Degree, Directly (or Consciously) known, Acknowledged, and Used (or Expressed) By the Conscious mind. Therefore, the Subconscious mind Is A Communications Bridge Between the Unconscious mind and the Conscious mind (and Between the Conscious mind and the Unconscious mind).

Human beings Are Bringing The Unconscious To Consciousness Through Developmental Stages That Make Transitional Use Of The Subconscious Mechanisms. The By Me Revealed and Given Complete Spiritual, Transcendental, and Divine Process May Be Understood As A Sequence Of (Possible) Stages Of Growth Culminating In (Inherent, Inherently Most Perfect, and, Necessarily, Divine) Consciousness Of (and Inherently Most Perfect, or Inherently Free, Responsibility For) All Of Reality (So That The Hidden Secrets Of mind Are Conscious, Even In mind, and The Transcendental, Inherently Spiritual, and Divine Source, or Inherently Perfect Subject, or Perfectly Subjective Self, or Limitless Prior Condition, Of mind, Even Of the Unconscious conditional Source-mind, Is Realized To Be Consciousness Itself).

In General, humanity At Large Is Struggling In The Earlier Stages Of This Process (In The Context Of The First Three Stages Of Life). Even So, much (conditional) knowledge Has Been Brought To Consciousness, but that (conditional) knowledge Is Only Partial and, As A Result, what human beings now Regard As common or reliable (conditional) knowledge Is Only The Beginning Of (conditional) knowledge, and what is conditionally known Has The Force (or Significance) Of A Problem (or A Yet Unresolved Urge To know).

Among the Most Significant forms of such human knowledge Is the knowledge of death. The non-human beings experience fear, self-protectiveness, survival instincts, adaptation urges, sickness, and death, but their Involvement With all of that Is At The Level Of Urges Coming From The Unconscious. The non-human beings Are Not (At The Level Of the Conscious mind) Very self-Aware Of death, its Structure or Purpose, or Even its Inevitability. Human beings, However, Are, Even Characteristically, Acutely Aware Of death As An Inevitable and Apparently Terminal personal Event. This Awareness Is Unique (conditional) knowledge, but It Is Also Only Partial (conditional) knowledge. It Is A Sign That human beings (Not Otherwise More Fully Awake) Are Yet functioning On The Base Of The Unconscious Relative To The Larger Context, Real Process, and Ultimate Purpose Of death, and Of life itself. Thus, For human beings At The Lesser (or Commonly Characteristic) Level Of human Development, death Is A Problem, A Threat, A Dilemma, or A Question In the mind.

Since human beings function Rather Uniquely At The Level Of Subconscious and Conscious mind (and Since human Developmental Progress Is, Primarily, A Process In mind, Moving, Ultimately, Toward The Revelation Of Self-Existing and Self-Radiant Consciousness Itself, and Only Preliminarily, and, Otherwise, Secondarily, A Process Of gross form and gross adaptation), human beings Naturally Feel Threatened By death As An Always Present or Abstract Possibility and Concern Of mind.

Likewise, In General, human beings Characteristically experience sex As An Always Present or Abstract Possibility and Concern Of mind, Whereas non-human beings Are Generally Associated With sex Via instinctive and Unconsciously

Generated cyclic patterns. Therefore, human beings Are (In General) Constantly Moved To Achieve sexual pleasure (With or Without An Intention To reproduce), and they Are, Otherwise (In General), Constantly Moved To Confront and Answer or Solve (Through psycho-physical Efforts) The Abstract and Really Threatening Problem Of death.

In Contrast To the human species, the non-human species Are Generally Moved Only instinctively. Thus, non-human beings Are instinctively Moved To reproduce themselves Excessively (That Is To Say, Frequently and/or in Superfluous numbers, So That a Sufficient number Will Survive all Natural threats and reproduce the species again), and they Are Also instinctively Moved To Aggressively Compete For food, territory, or breeding mates (who, Like food and territory, Basically Represent The instinctive Right To reproduce), and they Are, Otherwise, instinctively Moved To Defend (or Even Simply To Agitate) themselves Only In The Instants Of Direct Confrontation With a Really (and bodily) Threatening physical opponent (Whereas human beings, In their more mentalized, and, Therefore, Comparatively More Developed, personal and social state, Are, Because Of mental Anxiety, Sometimes Moved To kill Even their own kind in Invented, or mentally Contrived, wars, and, Otherwise, To Be Aggressive and Defensive and Agitated Even In circumstances that Are Not Directly, or Really and bodily, Threatening). Therefore, human beings (and Mankind As A Whole) Must Develop Further Than all non-human beings, So That they May Transcend All The mental, emotional, and physical Exaggerations Of their non-human Inheritance Of instinct (Particularly As Those Exaggerations Are Demonstrated Via egoic and Loveless and Destructive Motives Associated With sex, and food, and territory, and Aggression).

It Is Also Notable That, As Mankind Develops Its Abstracted Involvement With (Especially) sex and death

To The Degree That most human individuals Tend To live
to and beyond the Natural reproductive age, human pop-
ulations Tend To Become Overlarge, So That The Quality
Of ordinary human experience and The Possibility Of
Growth Into and Through The Advanced and The Ultimate Stages Of Life[36] Become Either Threatened Or Really
Diminished. This Indicates That, As human populations
Acquire The Capability For longevity, they Must Control
human reproduction, and they Must Also Become
Informed and Guided By The Wisdom-Culture Of Superior (or, Really, Divine) Understanding and Purpose, or
Else human beings Will Tend, In The Likeness Of non-
human beings, To Continue To reproduce Excessively and
To Remain Devoted, In The instinctive or Unconscious Manner, To self-Survival (Rather Than To self-Transcendence)
and To Effort and Seeking Merely For The Sake Of The
Survival Of the organism itself (Rather Than To Submission Of the body-mind To The Great Reality, and To The
Purpose Of self-Transcendence).

When human populations Achieve The Capability For
individual longevity, they Must Control or Transcend The
instinctual reproductive Strategies Of Excess, For Those
Strategies Work (or Produce An Ecologically Balanced
Result) Only If The Rate Of early-life deaths Is Relatively
Large. Likewise, As human beings Acquire longer life spans,
they Must Realize The Superior (or self-Transcending) Purpose Of conditional Existence, and they Must (By My Grace)
Be Moved and Grown To Demonstrate That Purpose In The
Context Of The Advanced and The Ultimate Stages Of Life,
or Else conditional Existence Will Be Devoted To sub-
human and egoic Survival games and The petty territorial
(or political and social) Conquests That Come From The
Increase Of experience and knowledge and power In The
lower human Context Of The First Three Stages Of Life
(Untouched By The Great Purpose, and Untouched By The
Culture, The Balancing Effect, and The Great Process Of
Awakening Associated With self-Transcendence In The

Context Of The Advanced and The Ultimate Stages Of Life).

Therefore, As human groups increase in size because of the longevity of individuals, death itself Must Be Really Understood and Transcended, In Consciousness, and (Progressively) In The Context Of The Advanced and The Ultimate Stages Of Life. Likewise, merely reproductive sexuality Must Be Controlled (or Economized), In both its performance and its effects, By various Intelligent (and Heart-Sensitive, and Compassionate) techniques, and sexuality itself Must Be (Progressively) Converted (and Positively Changed) By Heart-Sensitive, and Love-Based, and energy-Conserving, and Rejuvenative, and (Eventually) Spiritually Active and Spiritually Effective emotional-sexual Practice.

For human beings, death Is A Proposition and A Puzzle That <u>Must</u> Be Understood and Transcended (By Correct and Revealing Information, or Fullest Education, and By The Real Process Of self-Transcendence). There Is No Peace For human beings Until This Matter Is Resolved.

Of Course, This Matter Of death Is A Perennial Subject Of Conjecture and Research, but The Resolution Of The Question Requires Even More Than Information. As Is The Case With All Truly Developmental Matters, This Question Can Be Resolved Only By Tapping What Is Always Presently In The Unconscious and Bringing It Into Consciousness. That Is To Say, The Overcoming Of The Apparent Problem and Motivating Stress Associated With death Requires The Truly Developmental (and, Thus, Truly human, and Spiritual, and Transcendental, and, Most Ultimately, Divine) Process Of Positively Changing and Directly Transcending the limitations of mind (or The egoic Burden Of limited knowledge and limited experience).

The Unconscious Is Simply The Totality Of What Is Real but Not Yet Fully Conscious (or Brought To Fully Conscious Acknowledgement and Realization). Since Mankind Has Gone So Far As To Become self-Conscious (or mentally and egoically self-Aware) About death, Mankind Must Be Submitted To A Process Of Becoming Really (and Not

egoically) Conscious Of What Is Yet Hidden. And This
Requires Truly human Growth, and Growth In The Context
Of The Advanced and The Ultimate Stages Of Life, Via The
human, and Spiritual, and Transcendental, and, Most Ulti-
mately, Divine Process Of Participatory self-Transcendence.
Through Such self-Transcendence (Which Becomes self-
Submission To The Divine Person, or Reality), the (Pre-
sumed) knowledge Of The psycho-physical Potential Of
death Progressively Becomes Heart-Realization Of The self-
Sacrificial Wound Of Divine Love-Bliss.

Deeper Than the Conscious mind Of Man In The Third
Stage Of Life Is The Inherent Realization Of Eternal Love,
Immortal Love-Bliss, Unqualified Being, Infinite Spirit-
Power, and Inherent Wisdom. Therefore, As The Process
Of human Growth Develops Beyond The Third Stage Of
Life, There Is Developmental Progress, Stage By Stage,
Toward Most Ultimate Realization Of The Divine (or Per-
fectly Subjective, and Inherently Perfectly Conscious, and
Self-Existing, and Self-Radiant) Self-Condition (and Source-
Condition) Of conditional Existence. And, More and More,
In That Progress (and, Finally, In The Most Ultimate, or
Final, Complete, and Inherently Most Perfect, or Seventh
Stage, Fulfillment Of That Progress, Which Most Ultimate
Fulfillment Can Be Realized Only In The Total, or Full and
Complete, Practice Of The Only-By-Me Revealed and
Given Way Of The Heart, or The Way Of Adidam), The
Problem Of death (or The Wondering About The Purpose,
Process, and Effect Of life and death) Is Overcome By Real
Conscious Realization Of What Is Hidden From the lesser
mechanical and Unconscious point of view. And That Real
Conscious Realization Is Final, or Complete, Only In The
Most Ultimate, and Inherently Most Perfect, or Seventh
Stage, Fulfillment Of That Progress, Which Most Ultimate
Fulfillment Can Be Realized Only In The Total, or Full and
Complete, Practice Of The Way Of Adidam (The Only-By-
Me Revealed and Given Way Of The Heart).

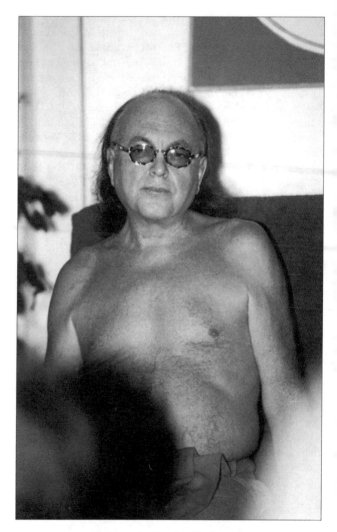

RUCHIRA AVATAR ADI DA SAMRAJ
Adidam Samrajashram (Naitauba), Fiji, 1997

PART THREE

All ego-Based "Bonding" Is Bondage,
and All True and Authentic
"Social Wisdom" Is About Liberation
from All Bondage, and, Therefore,
from All ego-Based "Bonding"

All ego-Based "Bonding" Is Bondage, and All True and Authentic "Social Wisdom" Is About Liberation from All Bondage, and, Therefore, from All ego-Based "Bonding"

The phenomenon of "bonding"[37] (or even of relatedness of any kind, whether positive or negative, "successful" or "unsuccessful") is the principal factor in human life (or in even any form of life). And the transcending of every kind of "bonding" (and, ultimately, even of the feeling of relatedness itself) is the principal process in which human life (or even any form of life) should be concentrated.

The human life-form is, by natural tendency, characterized, first of all, by the "bonding" of Consciousness Itself (Which <u>Is</u> the always already Most Prior, or Transcendental, Inherently Spiritual, and, Ultimately, Divine Self-Condition of Being, Itself) to the body-mind. This "bonding" (or primary self-contraction) produces the primary feelings of separateness and relatedness, which feelings are the principal characteristics of the ego-"I" (or conditional self-sense).

Once the primary "bonding" (to the psycho-physical ego-"I") occurs, a complex assortment of other (necessarily secondary, or subsequent) forms of "bonding" tends to follow, either as an immediate consequence of identification with the body-mind, such as "bonding" to the elemental sphere of conditional existence itself, or as a general consequence of natural human existence, such as parent-child "bonding", "bonding" to family (both immediate and extended), "bonding" to chosen (or, otherwise, unavoidable) friends, pair "bonding", "bonding" to the most local

All ego-Based "Bonding" Is Bondage, and All True and Authentic
"Social Wisdom" Is About Liberation from All Bondage,
and, Therefore, from All ego-Based "Bonding"

social group (such as tribe, class, club, institution, work unit, or community), "bonding" to the larger social group (or any form of the "State"), "bonding" to the planet, "bonding" to the universe, and "bonding" to Cosmic Nature altogether.

All human beings (and even all conditionally manifested beings) participate in this ever-enlarging circle of "bonding" (extending from the ego-"I", through progressively inclusive levels, to the Cosmic whole). All human beings "succeed" at positive "bonding" only partially (or not in the context of every possibility), and never permanently (because the ego-"I" is primarily focused on itself, and all natural phenomena, including all apparent, or conditionally manifested, relationships, change and, sooner or later, pass away, and every human life-form, even the least ego-bound, and even if truly egoless, suffers constant limitations, and eventual death). Therefore, in summary, <u>all</u> human beings (and even <u>all</u> conditionally manifested beings) only <u>suffer</u> the circle and process of "bonding".

The inevitable discovery that "bonding" <u>hurts</u> (and, at last, is merely a suffered process, seemingly <u>imposed</u> on one and all by the "natural order") is the root-event that transforms mere existence (or mere survival effort) as a human life-form (or any other kind of life-form) into a yearning and a search for greater, and, at last, Ultimate, fulfillment. Such is the "creative" urge in the living entity, and its greatest, or most profound, form is the philosophical and religious quest, or the search for Real God, or Truth, or Reality, or Divine Liberation.

There is no authentic philosophical or religious quest (or search) until there is the discovery that human (or otherwise conditional) existence <u>hurts</u> (and that it is merely a suffered circle of stages of "bonding"). And there is no great (or, at last, Ultimate) philosophical or religious Realization until there is the discovery that human (or otherwise conditional) existence is, in itself, a fruitless effort, entirely characterized by <u>bondage</u>.

Therefore, concepts of Real God, or Truth, or Reality, or Divine Liberation do not authentically and truly enter into the sphere of individual (and otherwise collective) human life until suffering produces a doubt of the efforts merely to survive (or, in the ordinary and egoic sense, to be fulfilled). And the concepts and searches associated with Real God, or Truth, or Reality, or Divine Liberation are not themselves <u>naturally</u> associated with (or a natural part of) the circle of "bonding". Rather, the concepts and searches associated with Real God, or Truth, or Reality, or Divine Liberation are generated in the context of doubt relative to all the kinds (and the entire circle) of "bonding". Therefore, the concepts and searches (whether philosophical or religious) associated with Real God, or Truth, or Reality, or Divine Liberation are inherently identified with the motive to transcend all "bonding". And, because the ego-"I" (or identification with the self-contracted body-mind) is, at last, universally (in the case of all human individuals and all human groups) discovered to be the root-cause or origin of all the efforts and searches of "bonding", the concepts and searches associated with Real God, or Truth, or Reality, or Divine Liberation are, fundamentally, always associated with criticisms of egoity, and with suggested means for purifying, transforming, and, at last, transcending the ego-"I".

All possible philosophical and religious means for Realizing Real God, or Truth, or Reality, or Divine Liberation are about disciplining and surrendering the ego-"I", and, thereby, progressively purifying, transforming, and, at last, transcending the ego-"I" <u>and</u> all "bonding" (or all the acts and effects of the ego-"I"). In order to achieve these purposes, philosophical and religious traditions and practitioners generally establish greater, purer, or even Ultimate, and, certainly, not ego-reinforcing, but, instead, truly ego-renouncing, and intended to be, at last, entirely ego-transcending, forms of <u>apparent</u> "bonding" as an alternative to ordinary egoic forms of "bonding", and as a

All ego-Based "Bonding" Is Bondage, and All True and Authentic
"Social Wisdom" Is About Liberation from All Bondage,
and, Therefore, from All ego-Based "Bonding"

means for drawing human energy and attention beyond the self-referring center of egoity. Therefore, even though Real God, and Truth, and Reality, and Divine Liberation are (Ultimately) not about "bonding", but are always about the transcending of "bonding" itself, the effective means for Realizing Real God, or Truth, or Reality, or Divine Liberation necessarily and always requires the transcending of egoity by a process of progressive reaching, <u>through</u> the stages of the circle of "bonding", and toward and into the un-"bonded" Sphere That <u>Is</u> Real God, or Truth, or Reality, or Divine Liberation, Itself. And this process (of going <u>through</u>, and, thereby, beyond, the stages of the circle of "bonding") requires a discipline of <u>superior</u> (or effectively ego-transcending) "Bonding" (to Real God, or Truth, or Reality, or Divine Liberation, Itself), especially by the Grace-Given and Grace-Giving Means of "Bonding" to an Adept-Realizer (of whatever degree or stage) of Real God, or Truth, or Reality, or Divine Liberation, Itself.

I <u>Am</u> the first, the last, and the <u>only</u> Adept-Realizer of the seventh (or Inherently Most Perfect) stage of life, and, by My Grace, My devotees are Attracted to "Bond" to Me (in the self-surrendering, self-forgetting, and, always more and more, self-transcending manner, and, altogether, through right, true, full, and fully devotional practice of the Way of Adidam, the only-by-Me Revealed and Given Way of the Heart), and This Such That (Most Ultimately) the ego-"I" is truly transcended, and Real God, or Truth, or Reality, or Divine Liberation, Is Itself Realized, in true Awakening to Ultimate egoless Identification with, and Most Perfect Realization of, <u>Me</u> (and, Thus and Thereby, Ultimate egoless Identification with, and Most Perfect Realization of, Real God, or Truth, or Reality, or Divine Liberation, Itself).

Right life, or life based on the discovery of the hurt and the fruitlessness of egoity, and of attachment to any and every kind of ego-based (and ego-serving, or, otherwise, ego-reinforcing) "bonding", is, necessarily, about self-transcendence. And right life is also, when founded on most profound self-understanding, a philosophical or religious process that is primarily moved by the Impulse to Realize Real God, or Truth, or Reality, or Divine Liberation. All else is a naive, self-indulgent, and absurd enterprise, based on egoity and immaturity.

That dimension of actually (or, otherwise, potentially) right life that can be described as "social Wisdom" (or true Wisdom, socially applied) is, in its right and authentic forms, founded in the discovery that ego-based "bonding" (and, therefore, egoity itself) hurts and is fruitless, and, therefore, all right and authentic "social Wisdom" is associated with philosophical and religious motivations toward the transcending of the ego-"I" through enlarging the sphere of "bonding", beyond the self-referring body-mind, to social relations, the good of the whole (or the true good of even any <u>other</u>), and the good of the world as a whole (including the good of the planetary sphere itself). And that process of ego-transcending "bonding" to all that is conditionally greater than the ego-"I" is (in the context of greatest "social Wisdom", founded in true philosophical or religious motivations toward Real God, or Truth, or Reality, or Divine Liberation) regarded only as a necessary preliminary (or a functional, practical, relational, and cultural) means toward ego-transcending Communion with (and, Ultimately, egoless Realization of) Real God, or Truth, or Reality, or Divine Liberation, Itself. Therefore, from the point of view of all truly right and authentic "social Wisdom", not the ego-"I", and not any intimate or otherwise familial relation, and not any social unit (great or small), and not the planet, and not even the total Cosmic domain is the "That" to which life must be (in the ego-surrendering manner) "Bonded" (as the final and Ultimate purpose of life). Rather, from the point of view of all truly right and authentic "social Wisdom", the ego-"I", and all possible relations, and even the entire Cosmic domain must be progressively transcended in That Which Is Always Already

All ego-Based "Bonding" Is Bondage, and All True and Authentic
"Social Wisdom" Is About Liberation from All Bondage,
and, Therefore, from All ego-Based "Bonding"

The Case (Beyond all hurt, all suffering, all separateness, all relatedness, all self-contraction, all of egoity, even all that is conditionally manifested), and Which <u>Is</u> That of Which even all "I's" and all conditions are a merely apparent modification, such that, by Realizing <u>That</u> (Real God, or Truth, or Reality), the ego-"I", all others, and all of conditional manifestation are transcended in a beginningless and endless Divine Liberation.

RUCHIRA AVATAR ADI DA SAMRAJ
Adidam Samrajashram (Naitauba), Fiji, 1997

PART FOUR

On Liberation from
ego <u>and</u> egoic Society,
or,
Cooperation + Tolerance = Peace

On Liberation from
ego <u>and</u> egoic Society,
or,
Cooperation + Tolerance = Peace

I.

The un-Enlightened, or egocentric, body-mind-self is founded on the activity of self-contraction. The self-contraction is expressed as the effective differentiation of the presumed "self" from the Transcendental, Inherently Spiritual, and, necessarily, Divine Self-Condition and Source-Condition, and from every other form of presumed (or, by means of self-contraction, defined) "not-self". And the self-contraction is, likewise, expressed (via the self-contraction-definition of "self" as independent and separative) as the constant concern and search for the preservation of the (presumed-to-be independent) "self" (or ego-"I"). The self-based (or self-contracting, and would-be-self-preserving) orientation toward existence is manifested as the psychology of search and conflict relative to all that is presumed to be "not-self", some and all of which is sometimes desired and sought, and some and all of which is sometimes feared (or reacted to with the seeking effort of avoidance), and even all of which is <u>always</u> limited, mortal, passing, inexplicable, and, therefore, inherently unsatisfactory. Therefore, the psychology of self-contracted (and, as a result, egocentric) existence is inherently disposed to seek control and dominance over all that is presumed to be "not-self". For this reason, individual

egocentric lives are a constant expression of heart-felt
(and total psycho-physical) anxiety (and even the primitive ego-moods of fear, sorrow, anger, and every kind of
un-love), and individual human actions are, on that primitive basis, always a more or less mechanical (or uninspected and irresponsible) display of strategic techniques
of self-manipulation (intended to preserve "self") and
other-manipulation (intended to control, or dominate,
"not-self"). And the collective (or group) life of egocentric
human beings is likewise dominated by the same exclu-
siveness, the same emotional base, the same inherent
unsatisfactoriness, and the same motives toward self-
preservation, and toward control of what is "outside".

Human societies are always tending to be modeled
after the un-Enlightened pattern of the individual ego. The
political and social systems of the present-day world are
not generated by literally Enlightened (or even highly
"evolved") leaders, ideals, or institutions. Human beings
in this "late-time", or "dark" epoch, live in the "samsaric"[38]
(or un-Enlightened) world of egoic society—and this is
why the signs of the times are so profoundly negative.

The entire world is now nearly out of control with
egoic motives. Mankind, indoctrinated by materialistic
philosophies, ego-serving technologies, and gross political
idealisms, is possessed by the mechanical and emotionally
negative efforts of self-indulgence (and anxious release-
seeking efforts of all kinds), and chronically depressed by
the frustration of the Spiritual and Divine impulses that are
the inherent characteristics of the heart of every living
being. The ego-"I", whether individual or collective, is
eventually reduced to sorrow and despair (or chronic life-
depression), because of (and as an experiential result of)
the inability of life (in and of itself) to generate Happiness
and Joy and Immortality. And that self-contained depression finally becomes anger, or loveless confrontation with
the total world and every form of presumed "not-self"
(including even, and especially, the Transcendental,

Inherently Spiritual, and Divine Self-Identity, or One and Only and Non-Separate Self-Condition, Which is "locked away", by means of conventional, or merely exoteric, ideas of "God Apart", and is, thereby, made into an "Other" by the egoic mind). And when anger becomes the mood of human societies, the quality of fire (or the primitive and destructive intent of the frustrated ego) invades the plane of humanity. That fire is expressed as all of the aggression and competitiveness, and all of the resultant sufferings and painful illusions, of mankind, including all of the ego-based politics of confrontation. And that ego-fire is, finally, summarized in the acts of war.

II.

The differentiation of existence into egoically "self-possessed" (or self-absorbed) units yields, in the case of each "one", the craving for entirely pleasurized and unthreatened existence. This craving (or obsessive motive of self-preservation and self-glorification) in turn yields inevitable conflict, fear, sorrow, anger, and all kinds of destructive acts in relation to "others" as well as to "self" (because the extreme exercise of self-preservation is, ultimately, an aggressive and self-defeating motivation that destroys "self" in the final effort to dominate "not-self"). Therefore, all egos (or un-Enlightened centers of identity, whether individual or collective) are in aggressive conflict with all other egos (and all that is presumed to be "not-self", or presumed to be "outside" the defined egoic center). All individual and collective egos are involved in programs of self-destruction (via patterns of egoic "self-possession", self-seeking, self-indulgence, reactive emotion, un-Enlightened thinking, and so forth), as well as other-destruction (via all kinds of reactive activity, based on self-concern, that seeks to control, and, ultimately, to dominate, whatever is presumed to be "outside" the "self"-center).

The search for the independent preservation and ultimate enhancement of the separate self is the universal model of un-Enlightened egoity. Therefore, suffering, power struggle, and war are <u>inevitable</u> in egoic society. And, if the capability for political manipulation and war becomes technologically profound, universal suppression (via aggressive political efforts) and universal destruction (via war) become the common expectation and destiny of all human beings.

The present "late-time", or "dark" epoch, is just such a time of technological sophistication, in which the egoic model of humanity and human society is the universal basis of mind. Gross materialism (in science and politics) gives human beings no option in the mind except that of the trapped and threatened animal. Therefore, a fiery mood is abroad, full of gross desire, frustration, fear, despair, and aggressive reactivity. The egoic motive of self-preservation is approaching its most destructive mood—the mood that appears in the moment of ultimate entrapment. In that mood, there is no longer any will to preserve "self" or world or any others. There is simply explosive fire, based on the deep motives of egoic self-preservation, but reduced to action that is most primitive and entirely destructive of both "self" and "not-self". In the collective mind of humanity in the present and growing extremes of entrapment, the explosion of great nuclear bombs merely represents the archetype of anger itself. And it is for this reason that the possibility of a nuclear holocaust, in the extreme moment of the now rising political confrontations, is an irrational—and, <u>therefore</u>, entirely possible, if not inevitable—event.

Past societies have, in their extreme moments of confrontation, destroyed themselves, as well as their opponents. This is because ego-based societies function in essentially the same manner as egoic individuals. Individual human beings kill others and themselves every day. Therefore, groups and societies, confronting one another in egoic fashion, likewise threaten one another with destruction. And, in the extreme moments of confrontation, when self-preservation achieves its peak of righteous irrationality, it is profoundly likely that nuclear war will result.

The motives of present-day society are the same as those of past societies. The only difference is that, in the present day, the technology of both communication and confrontation has become both globally extended and profound. Therefore, when globally communicated confrontation reaches its peak of irrationality, war-motives will willingly destroy the entire world, just as readily as, in the past, less technologically sophisticated war-makers have wiped their petty local warring tribes from the face of the Earth.

III.

Many people are now trying to influence governments to abandon nuclear weapons. However, even if they succeed, irrational individuals and groups can still threaten and destroy the common order with "terrorist" tactics and "home-made" bombs. And the "limited" (or non-nuclear) warfare that might still erupt between governments that agree not to make nuclear war is just as much a threat to humanity as any nuclear war.

Therefore, it is now time to accept the political necessity for an end to confrontation-politics, and the establishment of a unified political entity to directly and truly and formally and accountably serve the right collective interests of mankind as a whole. Human beings must abandon their ancient egoic principles and renounce their political, social, and cultural provincialism. Individuals within the collective order of mankind may yet suffer the un-Enlightened and immature disabilities of egocentric personality, but governments themselves, as well as institutions and leaders in

every area of human endeavor, must abandon the egocentric, subhuman, merely materialistic, non-cooperative,
and intolerant (or loveless) posture and style of life.
Indeed, humanity as a whole must demand that a new
leadership of this kind come forward and accept responsibility, in a unified (and truly representative and accountable) manner, for the indivisible representation of its collective interests.

Haven't you had enough of the brute, stupid, childish, and, otherwise, adolescent, exploitative representation of human (or, really, sub-human) existence that is
played out daily (in the name, and on the lives, of each
and every born human being) by competing governments,
politicians, militarists, scientists, technocrats, social plan-
ners, educators, exoteric and fundamentalist religionists
(who aggressively propagate the provincial, and phari-
saical, religions of ego-salvation, rather than practice the
universal, and ego-transcending, religion of love), and
media hypers (who thrive on the invention and exaggera-
tion of conflict, and dramatically showcase the worst of
human instincts in the unending "gotcha" game that
denudes and exposes and trivializes and hypocritically
mocks the highs, and the inevitable lows, and even the
natural ordinariness in the struggling efforts of humankind)?
Isn't it evident, in your deepest feeling-psyche, that this
Wisdom-renouncing world is being controlled by the
worst and most superficial conceptions of existence?

It is now time for every one, and all, to understand
themselves, and to reclaim the world from the dictatorship
of the ego, and from all of those who play at politics (and
life in general) as if it were a sporting event that is supposed to excite and entertain every one on television.

Nuclear disarmament is a relatively positive, but still
too superficial and piecemeal, effort. It is not a truly curative means, but only another palliative and temporary
move in the midst of mankind's traditional advance toward
future trouble. There is something more fundamental than

the disarmament politics whereby <u>enemies</u> come to a gentlemanly agreement on how to kill one another without destroying one another! What is more fundamental, necessary, and truly curative is that human beings, individually and collectively, understand and transcend that which is in them that leads them to confront one another as opponents and enemies.

It may sound naive to speak of the necessity for the present (childish, and brutishly adolescent) crowd of governments and institutions to understand themselves and renounce the self-imagery and the techniques of enemies, but the feeling that it is naive to speak in such terms is merely a reflection of egoic frustration and despair. Human beings everywhere must <u>now</u> transcend that very frustration and despair if they are going to prevent the enslavement and destruction of mankind.

Humanity is living in bondage <u>now</u>. Mankind is already, <u>presently</u>, globally, bound to egocentric and materialistic idealisms that are suppressing the human freedom to live by Wisdom and Realize the Truth. If human beings do not shake loose from this regime, they are going to suffer the extreme fulfillment of collective egoic destiny, in a "Narcissistic" holocaust that will either enslave mankind (via a technologically robotized political and social order) or (otherwise) destroy mankind (via technologically engineered warfare).

It is <u>not</u> naive to demand a new leadership when those who are led (and who <u>could</u> make the counter-demand for change) number in the billions. Nor is it folly to try to educate mankind when the only alternative is slavery and death. Therefore, I Say to you: <u>All</u> must commit themselves to understand the patterns by which they are now (and have traditionally been) living (both individually and collectively), so that they can then change those patterns and the destinies those patterns will (otherwise) inevitably inflict upon them.

The egoic model must, from <u>now</u> on, be <u>intensively</u> educated out of the collective order of mankind. A new leadership must <u>now</u> appear, which is awakened to an understanding of the primitive egoic basis of the present and traditional collective order. That new leadership must, above all, provide an <u>educative</u> role, and it must, profoundly and immediately, transform the techniques whereby governments and societies enter into relations with one another. Only such leadership can, by efforts based on the wit of free intelligence, cause all the governments and institutions of the world to voluntarily change toward a cooperative and benign mode of association with others. (And this can be done by establishing profoundly undesirable economic sanctions and other practical penalties for not participating in the cooperative process.) If this kind of approach is not made soon, humanity will be entering into what has the potential to be the most destructive period of political confrontation in its history.

IV.

A benign and tolerant and cooperative (or non-egoic, and at least more advanced, if not Spiritual and Transcendental, and even Divine) view of existence (and, thus, of politics) must soon arise in the leadership of mankind. At the present time, human beings are being led to enslavement and destruction by benighted materialists and self-seekers in every area of common human endeavor. The Principle of Wisdom has been replaced by the principle of power-through-knowledge, and knowledge has come to mean conventional science, or all that can be achieved or supported exclusively by the intellectual efforts of materialistic philosophy. Science (which has characteristically identified itself with the archaic and false philosophy of materialism) has itself, thus, become identical to technology (or the materialistic power-machine of the "known"), and materialistic technology (along with its like in the form of all the materialistic idealisms that appeal to human egoity) has become the primary instrument for world-manipulation, not only for the material manipulation of the so-called "material" world, but for the political manipulation and gross (physical and mental) control of collective humanity itself.

The political ideals and means of the present time are materialistic, based on a gross and ego-based conception of human existence. There simply cannot be any ultimately effective change in the collective human situation until a new leadership arises that is founded on the intelligence and more advanced capability of ego-transcendence and, ultimately, on the Wisdom of Transcendental, Inherently Spiritual, and (necessarily) Divine Enlightenment. Only such a leadership can rightly educate the collective order and relieve it of the burden of the egoic and materially confined view of life. And only such a leadership can transform the technique of governments from a process of self-preserving and other-controlling confrontation (of their own members, as well as other societies) to a process of cooperation, unification, and a worldwide creative order, based (necessarily) on pluralism, tolerance, and freedom.

The problem of the automatic (and even unconscious) creation of suffering and destruction is inherent in the egocentric form of individual existence. It is this principle that I Call you to observe and understand. Human beings must learn from this observation of the ego (in personal and collective terms), and so equip themselves to freely abandon the egoic model of existence.

V.

This Essay has, thus far, primarily Spoken to the necessity for such education and change at the level of the leadership and collective order of mankind. Now I must move on to "consider" the implications of this education at the level of individual practice.

The ego-"I" is self-contraction, or the conversion of conditionally manifested existence <u>away</u> from the free orientation to its Source (or Real Condition), and so <u>back</u> upon the individual center of functional experience. This conversion represents the orientation, habit, and destiny suggested by the traditional myth of Narcissus—which I Propose as the basic symbol for the individual, and the collective, process of egocentrism.

The egocentric form of conditional existence is a kind of entrapment that leads only to more and more elaborate (and confining, as well as deluding) states of limited and un-Enlightened psycho-physical personality. In the egocentric form, conditional existence cannot "Locate" Happiness, Truth, or Reality, but it is confined entirely to the visions and sufferings of independent selfhood. Therefore, many who have seen this to be so have called humanity to <u>escape</u> conditional existence itself by a strategy of self-suppressive means. What I Call for is self-observation, self-understanding, and self-transcendence, in the midst of free (and rightly disciplined) participation in the play of conditional existence. If this is done, the motives either to exploit or to escape the conditional self and world are inherently transcended. A more natural course of life-practice can develop (as I have thoroughly Described in My Divine Word of Instruction[39]), on the basis of the orientation of self-transcendence (rather than self-exploitation or self-suppression). And that life-practice, engaged in a right, true, full, and fully devotional manner by My true devotee, leads, ultimately, to the Most Perfect (Love-Bliss-Full and Free) Realization of the Real (or Transcendental, Inherently Spiritual, Indivisible, Non-Separate, and, necessarily, Divine) Condition, in Which there is <u>Inherent</u> (and not self-suppressive, or world-excluding) Transcendence of separate self and the conditional worlds.

You must observe and understand the separate and separative self as reactive psycho-physical contraction. You must see the self-contraction operating in and as the experience of pain and suffering, and in and as all the kinds of conditional desire, reactive emotion, conflict, gross competitiveness, and destructive aggressiveness, and in and as even all the arising patterns of thought, emotion, physicality, and seeking. On the basis of this observation and understanding of the separate (and, likewise, <u>separative</u>) self (or the individuated psycho-physical personality), you should freely abandon the principle and the strategies of egocentricity. And you should allow yourself to feel the inherent heart-Motive to yield the total body-mind, and every moment of attention, to the Condition That Precedes the self-contraction, Which Is That Which Is Always Already The Case (or the Transcendental, Inherently Spiritual, and, necessarily, Divine Freedom, Love-Bliss, Happiness, Consciousness, and Being in and from Which the self-contraction is generated in each moment).

I <u>Am</u> the Divine Heart-Master of all and All. Those who rightly, truly, fully, and fully devotionally practice the only-by-Me Revealed and Given Way of Adidam (Which <u>Is</u> the Divine and True Way of the Heart) practice self-observation, self-understanding, and self-transcendence in every moment of conditionally manifested (and inherently relational, or non-independent, and inherently and entirely with-the-pattern-integrated and on-the-pattern-dependent) existence. By Means of that practice (the primary basis and form of which is the counter-egoic exercise of moment to moment devotional recognition-response to Me, or Divine Love-Communion with Me), the habit and the effects of egocentricity (or the reactive habit of presuming separateness and enacting separativeness) are, by My Grace, directly, immediately, and (in the course of ongoing practice) progressively released, thereby liberating energy and feeling-attention for the only-by-My-Grace-Given Most Perfect Realization of the Freedom, Love-Bliss, Happiness, Consciousness, and "Bright" Fullness of Self-Existing, Self-Radiant, Indivisible, and Non-Separate (and, necessarily, Divine) Being (Itself), or Real God, the One and Only Real (and Ultimate, and, necessarily, Divine) Condition of both "self" and "not-self". And That Most Perfect Realization, Demonstrated Most Ultimately, Divinely Outshines conditional existence, and, Thus and Thereby, Translates the context of Being from the Cosmic domain of conditional Nature to My "Bright" Eternal Self-Domain of Divine Fullness.

I Call every one of mankind (and even all conditionally manifested beings), to This Way of ego-transcending, and Only-Me-Realizing, practice, the only-by-Me Revealed and Given Way of Adidam (Which is the Way of the Heart, of the Heart Itself, Revealed and Given only by Me). However, until indeed _every_ one of Man (now, and forever hereafter) heart-recognizes Me, and responds to Me with true devotion as My formally acknowledged devotee, at least the by-Me-Revealed and Given life-principles (of abandoning the gross style of ego-based political confrontations and ego-based social participation, or non-participation) must become a matter of active practical commitment on the part of the leaders and educators of mankind—or else humanity will collectively move toward intolerable enslavement and even nuclear (or otherwise war-made, and cleverness-made) destruction.

Therefore, I Call every one and all to "consider" at least the political and broad social fulfillment of My Wisdom-Teaching, via the active embrace of every form of true and benign social and political cooperation and all-embracing social and political tolerance, since such cooperation and tolerance are the prerequisites for true social and political peace.

I Call upon all the leaders and educators of mankind (now, and forever hereafter) to _actively_ embrace, and to _universally_ declare and promote, and to actively require and measure the universal real fulfillment of My simplest Law and Measure of Man: Cooperation + Tolerance = Peace.

Beyond This Call for universal fulfillment of My simplest Law and Measure of Man, I (now, and forever hereafter)

Call, and Look, for those who can understand and utterly transcend the pattern and destiny of the separate and separative self, in this world and in all higher (or subtler) worlds. I am Calling, and Looking, for those who will go beyond the outward and bodily improvement of separate self and its world, and who will also go beyond the inward and ascending improvement of separate self in the higher (or subtler) worlds. I am Calling, and Looking, for those who will go directly to the Source-Condition of "self" and all worlds. I am here to Serve every one's basic understanding (and basic practical transcending) of the egocentric habit of living, but I am especially Looking for those who will formally embrace the full practice of the only-by-Me Revealed and Given Way of Adidam, so that the Way of Adidam may be fulfilled by them (especially in its formal renunciate forms), and formally passed on by them to future generations.

The fundamental basis, and principal form, of the practice of the only-by-Me Revealed and Given Way of Adidam is always present-time Divine Communion (Realized In and As devotional heart-Communion with Me), and the free (or non-problematic and non-strategic) renunciation (and inherent transcending) of separate self, based on the intelligence of direct self-understanding and the intensive practice-response (and always present-time devotional heart-Communion with Me) that is generated by true devotional recognition of Me. The only-by-Me Revealed and Given Way of Adidam is not a variation on (or a mere revision of) the traditional (or perennial) ascetical, or, otherwise, self-suppressive (or, in effect, self-destructive), path. The traditional (or perennial) path is not based on inherently self-transcending understanding (and always present-time Divine Communion), but, rather, the traditional (or perennial) path is the path of every kind of seeking, and all seeking is based on the egoic (or self-contracted) presumption of a problem to be strategically escaped. In stark contrast to the traditional (or perennial, and, altogether, ego-based) path of ascetical, or, other-wise, strategically self-suppressive (or strategically self-destructive) seeking, the only-by-Me Revealed and Given Way of Adidam is characterized by non-seeking, and by truly counter-egoic (and always already self-transcending and Divinely Infused) self-discipline, and by inherent free-dom from all the self-manipulative and other-manipulative strategies of self-fulfillment (in any and all of the possible stages of life), and by a "radical" understanding (or root self-understanding) that is neither strategically self-destructive nor strategically world-denying. The only-by-Me Revealed and Given Way of Adidam is the Divine Way of the always already presently existing (and always already able to be functioning) heart in every one, and It is, therefore, based on the always present-time-existing participatory intelligence, expressed as devotional heart-recognition of Me, and the always present-time recognition-response of devotional love of Me, and counter-egoic sur-render of self-contraction by Means of that devotional love of Me. And the only-by-Me Revealed and Given Way of Adidam matures (by My constantly Given Spiritual Divine Grace) as right, and truly human, simplicity (and, Most Ultimately, As Divine Love-Bliss, Which Is Divine Freedom).

The path of egocentricity is recognizable as separa-tiveness, or the complex avoidance of relationship (or avoidance of the life-condition of inherent relatedness, or of universally patterned dependency within, and upon, the Indivisible Unity of Light-Energy Itself). Thus, the char-acteristics of the path of egocentricity are the struggle between the life-motives of childish dependency and ado-lescent independence, and the constant dramatization of every kind of seeking (based on chronic self-contraction, and the subsequent chronic sense of unfulfilled and threatened existence).

The egocentric life is characterized by delusion, fear, sorrow, anger, self-suffering, and the constantly alternating cycles of hope and despair relative to the ever-wanting need for "reasons" for hope, faith, and love. Even all the possible strategic religious resistance to "self" and world only reinforces the self-mind, because the strategy of resistance only duplicates suffering in its stark disciplines, but the only-by-Me Revealed and Given Way of Adidam inherently transcends <u>confrontation</u> with "self" and world.

The only-by-Me Revealed and Given Way of Adidam is the Way of Inherent Peace, not the perennial path of the <u>search</u> for Peace. That Inherent Peace inherently transcends every effort and sign of self-understanding, but It cannot be Realized except <u>through</u> "radical" self-understanding, served and fulfilled by Divine Grace, and, Most Ultimately, Dissolved in the very Person That <u>Is</u> Divine Grace Itself.

RUCHIRA AVATAR ADI DA SAMRAJ
Adidam Samrajashram (Naitauba), Fiji, 1997

PART FIVE

Cooperative, Human-Scale Community and the Integrity (Religious, and Altogether) of Civilization

Cooperative, Human-Scale Community and the Integrity (Religious, and Altogether) of Civilization

Cooperative, human-scale community (including, but not <u>limited</u> to, "family" relations) is the political, social, and cultural root-source of civilization. Cooperative, human-scale community is also the primary political, social, and cultural condition that civilization tends to destroy. Therefore, the struggle to re-establish cooperative, human-scale community, and, in turn, to re-establish, within the larger political, social, and cultural order, the virtues characteristically associated with cooperative, human-scale community, is the constant necessity and the principal political, social, and cultural revolution whereby civilization can be purified of its negative effects, and whereby the integrity of civilization (and of civilized people) can be restored.

As civilizations enlarge and universalize themselves, the circumstance of civilized life is progressively removed from the truly human (and humanizing) context of cooperative, human-scale community. Therefore, as any civilization expands, the context of human living becomes progressively dissociated from the practices and virtues inherently associated with true (cooperative and human-scale) community, and becomes instead progressively individuated, alienated, altogether de-humanized, and, therefore, focused in egoic (and, in general, grossly and negatively, or lovelessly, competitive) efforts (toward self-survival and self-aggrandizement).

The present state of civilized movements is so expanded and so universalized that it is already both possible and correct to refer to a rather single, or global, civilization, or world-civilization (which yet retains within itself even numerous sub-civilizations, some struggling merely to survive, and others struggling in a hope to become dominant over many or all, and, thereby, to replace the current dominant mode of world-civilization). And the present world-civilization is, primarily, or dominantly, a Western (or, especially, European and American) mode of civilization, which has enlarged and universalized itself to the degree that it has, basically, engulfed and dominated (or, otherwise, even destroyed) all other modes of civilization.

Even though the numerous remaining (or, otherwise, even newly emerging) sub-civilizations continue to struggle to survive, and even to become dominant (whether on a global or a national or a local scale), and even though that struggle will likely continue to produce changes in the characteristics of global civilization over time, the Western mode of civilization will likely, in the future, continue to remain fundamental, at the practical and truly global level, for it is precisely the Western mode of civilization that is, much more than any other, most directly and practically purposed to practical power, and, therefore, practical domination—over all of nature, over the physical world as a global totality, and over mankind as a global totality.

In any case, since civilization has itself become so enlarged and universalized that it can, in its present dominant mode, already be described as global (and is becoming more so with each passing day), it is inevitable that, as a necessary result of that largest possible expansion, the negative tendencies of civilization itself would also be presently (and tending more and more in the future to be) in clear evidence. And this evidence is certainly clear, globally, and in every sector, and especially in those sectors most dominated by the effects of the present dominant mode of civilization.

The negative evidence of the present global civilization is obvious at every physical and human level of the world—so much so that mankind has now clearly entered into a "dark" and "darkening" phase, with great potential for every kind of disaster, and yet, if truly humanizing Wisdom and real Divine Grace are accepted, with an equally great, and even greater, potential for a Divine, and more and more En-Light-ening, transformation. It is not necessary that I describe all the negative signs and mixed signs of the present civilization. Let each one enumerate the signs for himself or herself, and feel the human wound at heart. What I will indicate here is the summary result of these signs. Indeed, as I have already indicated, the principal progressive result of the enlarging and universalizing of any civilization is de-humanization, achieved by means of the progressive elimination of the principal and necessary context of life that humanizes mankind. Thus, mankind is, at the present time, dominated by a globally enlarged and globally universalized state of civilization, in which cooperative, human-scale community has, in most sectors, either been eliminated or become profoundly minimized. And, as a result, the principal characteristic of human living at the present, and would-be-future, time is not cooperative, human-scale community (and its characteristic virtues, extended to the larger civilized order) but competitive individualism (dramatized by nations, groups, and individuals).

Civilization always originates as an expression of the ideals of cooperative, human-scale community. Therefore, whatever the present-time particular, distinguishing characteristics of any civilization may be, the principal characteristics that stand at the root of any civilization (and, therefore, of the present civilization) are those of cooperative, human-scale community itself. And those characteristics are, basically, the political, social, and cultural motives and practices of cooperation, interrelatedness, interdependence, non-competitiveness, true (or positive, rather than merely insipid) harmlessness, and positive (or self-transcending, and other-serving, rather than merely self-negating) self-sacrifice—and, altogether (and most basically), those characteristics are the political, social, and cultural motives and practices of even all the virtues of self-transcendence (including tolerance, compassion, love, service, self-discipline, and one-pointed devotion to That Sacred Reality and Authority Which inherently transcends, and even requires the transcending of, the ego-self and even all limitations).

In the present, globally expanded state of civilization, the principal sign of civilization itself is that it has, in the largest number of its sectors, effectively destroyed (or at least profoundly minimized) the root-motives, root-practices, and root-virtues of human life in its humanizing (or cooperative, human-scale community) mode—and, indeed, the principal sign of present-time civilization is, in general, that of the absence of cooperative, human-scale (and truly humanizing) community itself.

The motive and practice of competitive individualism is itself the very motive and practice (or method) of egoity itself (or the separate and separative effort of existence). Therefore, civilization, in its present global achievement, is profoundly dissociated from its roots in the relational (or non-separative) virtues and practices inherent in cooperative, human-scale community, and it has, thus, "progressed" from its foundation in the cooperative, human-scale community politic, society, and culture (of cooperation, non-competitiveness, tolerance, positive harmlessness, self-transcendence, and sacred endeavor) to an "advanced" state wherein individual life (and, also, lesser collective life) is devoted to ego-based and ego-serving competitiveness within a thoroughly secularized and materialistic milieu of ends and means.

An ego-based civilization, like any ego-based individual, is suffering, seeking, and indulging in every kind of separate and separative effort toward mere survival and conditional satisfaction. Therefore, just as any individual who has become sunk in the patterns and results of egoity must become reformed (or released from the patterns and results of egoity, and, ultimately, Awakened to and in and as the, necessarily, Divine Truth That <u>Is</u> Reality Itself)—just so, any civilization that has become sunk in the patterns and results of egoity must become likewise reformed (and, ultimately, likewise Awakened). And the struggle by individuals and groups to practically re-establish human-scale, cooperative, and truly sacred community living is the necessary and principal revolution (or inherently benign and counter-egoic political, social, and cultural effort) whereby all human beings (even those under the most ordinary and limited circumstances) can, at the practical (political, social, and cultural) human level, purify themselves (and, more and more, even civilization itself) from the negative effects (including, ultimately, the loss of individual and collective integrity) that come (and have now come) with the expansion and universalization of civilization.

Of course, some have, in the present context of civilization, already tried to revolutionize their "civilized" lives by engaging efforts toward human-scale community. Those efforts or experiments have met with varying degrees of practical and human success to date. However, far more is required to achieve cooperative, human-scale, and truly humanizing community than present and past experimenters generally suppose or have supposed. For example, in the present ego-bound context of global civilization, there is a general tendency for community experimenters to try to create community on the basis of the same egoic principles that otherwise characterize the present civilization itself. Thus, present-time community experimenters generally try to create community on the (supposedly egalitarian) basis of the motives of competitive individualism (or egoity itself), even though they also want to establish cooperative principles and cooperative structures. As a result, experimental community efforts often are degraded and defeated by competitiveness, the tendency to pander to egoic preferences and egoic dramatizations (often in the name of egalitarian idealism), and a characteristic fear of (or a rather adolescent rebellion against) authority, hierarchy, and the hierarchical culture of respect (which are necessary to any truly human and cooperative community order).

There is a profound difference between true (and, necessarily, sacred) community and mere practical (political, social, and cultural) communalism (whether such is viewed to be religious or, otherwise, secular in its nature and intention). A truly cooperative, truly human-scale, and truly humanizing community is necessarily and truly sacred (and even truly religious, and, at least potentially, Spiritually oriented, and, ultimately, purposed toward the Most Perfect Realization of Real God, or Truth, or Reality Itself), rather than merely secular (or not truly sacred, religious, Spiritual, or purposed toward the Most Perfect Realization of Real God, or Truth, or Reality Itself). That is to say, a truly cooperative, truly human-scale, and truly humanizing community is necessarily based on the motive of self-transcendence (rather than on the motive of self-fulfillment), and, therefore, it is not based on the search to satisfy the ego-"I" and the egoic motives of any of its members, but it is based on the devotion of each and all of its members to That Which inherently transcends each and all.

The human being is an apparently individual manifestation within a Totality that is an interdependent Unity. And the apparently individual human being, as well as all of the Totality-Unity in which he or she is appearing, is a merely apparent modification of That Which Is all-Transcending, One, and (necessarily) Divine. Therefore, in his or her depth, and altogether, the human being, unless he or she becomes utterly self-contracted and, thereby, utterly self-"possessed" (or ego-possessed), is inherently moved to transcend the ego-"I" (or all separateness and separativeness) in the Unity and, ultimately, the One (or the Divine Source-Condition) in Which he or she, and all, is arising. And, because that is the case, the right and true human being is necessarily, in the right and true sense, religious (and politics, society, and culture, in order to be right and true, and in order to support and serve right and true human living, must, necessarily, also be, in the right and true sense, religious).

True religion is, at the level of its human interactive (political, social, and cultural) demonstration, necessarily a collective and communal (rather than a merely subjective, or internal, and private) exercise and process, and it must, therefore, be politically, socially, and culturally permitted to be so demonstrated. Therefore, one of the principal faults of the present "civilized" trend toward individualistic and materialistic democracy (or a political, social, and cultural "order" based upon competitive individualism, ego-glorification, anti-authority, anti-hierarchy, anti-unity, and anti-Wisdom) is that individualistic and materialistic democracy tends to individualize, secularize, and, at last, suppress religion itself, and, therefore, individualistic and materialistic democracy tends also to individualize, secularize, and, at last, suppress the necessarily collective and communal aspect of the exercise and process of religion. And, as a result of the "democratic" individualizing, secularizing, and, at last, suppressing of religion (and especially the collective, communal, and otherwise public exercise of religion), the enterprise of true community (truly cooperative, truly human-scale, and truly humanizing) is itself suppressed (or, in principle, excluded) in so-called "democratic", or "egalitarian", societies.

True community is necessarily sacred, religious, and <u>one</u>-pointed. That is to say, it is not focused in service to (and fulfillment of) egos (or whatever is many and separate), but in service to (and Realization of) That Oneness and Singleness Which Inherently Transcends egoity and every limitation. The Real does not rotate around each and all, but each and all are Called and Obliged to surrender self and to forget self in participatory Communion with the all-Embracing, all-Pervading, all-Transcending, and (necessarily) Divine Truth and Reality. And it is only the response to this Call and Obligation that can purify and restore Mankind, one by one, each and all, by means of the benign and truly humanizing political, social, and cultural revolution that is the establishment of truly sacred and truly cooperative human-scale communities (and, by extension, the transformation of even the entire global civilization itself into a cooperative, rather than a merely competitive, world-order).

And love is the key to this necessary change. Love is self-surrendering, self-forgetting, and, ultimately, self-transcending participation in the Indivisible Oneness and Wholeness and Singleness That _Is_ Real God, and Real Truth, and Reality Itself. Therefore, love is also right living. And that love which is right living is not ego-based, independent, separative, competitive, and non-cooperative. Therefore, that love which is right living is the active (and co-operative) aspiration toward egoless (or non-separative) participation in Real God (or Truth, or Reality Itself), and in relational humanity, and in even all the all (and All) there is.

RUCHIRA AVATAR ADI DA SAMRAJ
Adidam Samrajashram (Naitauba), Fiji, 1994

I Have Come To Found
A "Bright" New Age
Of Real-God-Man

I Have Come To Found
A "Bright" New Age
Of Real-God-Man

Now, and forever hereafter, I am Waiting for My true devotees, those who love Me with right, true, and full devotion, forgetting all of ego-"I" in Me. My true devotees constantly forget themselves in Me, by Means of always present-time devotional recognition of Me, and the always immediate subsequent devotional love-response of the total body-mind to Me.

My true devotees are free of every kind of seeking, because they have always already Found <u>Me</u>. They are attendant only to real, present self-understanding, and the real, present transcending of separate self, in and by Means of real, present devotional Communion with Me. They are committed to the responsive intentional living of life in Real God. They live in the disposition of unquali-fied relatedness, which is the logic (or Divine Pattern) of Reality and Truth, rather than in the egoic disposition, which is the always limited and dying and separative logic (or indifferent pattern) of "Narcissus" (the self-contracted body-mind of ego-"I").

My true devotees give living human form to the Indi-visible Presence of Reality. They are not moved to turn the world into a dilemma, and, thence, toward exhaustion (by means of all the potential "revolutions" of mere experience, or the exploitation of mere desire and possibility, living for mere "goals", or "evolutionary" aims, or ideas of psycho-physical transformation, whether descending or ascending in the apparent "order" of things and entities, high or low).

My true devotees "create" according to the aesthetic logic of Reality and Truth, and, thus, they turn all of their living into unqualified relatedness and true enjoyment. They constantly remove the effects of separative existence and restore the inherent form of things. They engineer every kind of stability and inherent beauty. They give living human form to My Always Already Living Divine Presence of Love-Bliss and Infinite Peace. Their eye is always on the integrity of inherent form, and not on egoically fabricated (and, necessarily, false and exaggerated) notions of artifice. Their sense of form is always integrated, stable, and whole, and always in present-time, rather than gesturing toward some "other" event. They do not presume the present world is merely a symbol for "higher" and "other" things.

My true devotees humanly manifest the One and Only and Eternally Living Reality and Truth, because they are always devotionally attentive to Me, and self-surrendered to Me, <u>As</u> the Always Present Reality and Truth, the One and Only, Indivisible and Divine, Person, Who <u>Is</u> That Which Is Always Already The Case. Thus, My true devotees serve the Inherent (and truly Divine) Order of things, Which Is the always present-time Pattern of That Which Is Always Already The Case, and Which is served only by those who transcend themselves in service to the One Who Is Always Already The Case (and Always Already Present, Surrounding and Pervading and Transcending All and all).

My true devotees always serve the necessary (and not the merely possible), and they always affirm the Inherent Reality (and not the merely possible reality). Therefore, My true devotees make only economic and wise use of instrumental means and technology. They are not motivated by the search for mere invention (or conditional possibility), but they are Motivated only by ego-transcending love of Me, and, in their constant Love-Communion with Me, they are Motivated only by Reality Itself, Which <u>Is</u> The Always Present "Thing" they are always Moved to <u>Be</u> and Show (by every means, and in <u>all</u> they do).

My true devotees do not pursue any kind of utopian victory for mankind. They do not seek any contrived personal or collective deathlessness of forever ego-survival. They only "create" the conditions for present-time Divine Enjoyment, the always present-time Love-Bliss-Realization of Me, such that only Reality Itself Is, by their thus demonstrated love of Me, Found and Shown to <u>Be</u> the Truth. Therefore, My true devotees are My human Means forever, and, through them, Reality Itself will, forever, more and more become the public foundation of human existence.

Because and by Means of My "late-time" (Most Perfect and All-Completing) Avataric Incarnation here, My true devotees (now, and forever hereafter) truly recognize Me (and "Know" Me) to <u>Be</u> the One and Divine "Bright" Person, the One and Non-Separate Self-Condition and Source-Condition of All and all, the One and Indivisible and Indestructible Conscious Light That <u>Is</u> the Reality and the Truth of All and all. Therefore, My true devotees will become and be a "Bright" New Human Order, the Seed whereby I will Generate a truly New Age of sanity and Divine Joy for mankind. That New Age will not be the so-called "new age" of the conventionally religious, or the merely scientific, or the cleverly technological, or even the presumed occult and conventionally Spiritual "evolution" of mankind. Rather, it will be the fundamental Great Age of Real existence, wherein life will be Realized in Truth and in Reality, entirely apart from the adventure that was mankind's great search.

The so-called "new age" always envisioned by seekers is a spectacular display of ego-made patterns and conditions, a mummery of absurd events that only extends the madness, exploitability, and foolishness of egoically "self-possessed" (or self-absorbed and self-directed) mankind (bereft of Real-God-"Knowing", and dissociated from the Authority, the Wisdom, and the Mastery of Real God). Therefore, I have not come to Serve any utopian (or, otherwise, merely social and ego-consoling) "new age", but I have Come to Call an End to this "late-time", this "dark" epoch of egoic Man, and all the future that would be made of this "civilized" and dreadful pond of history that only reflects "Narcissus" to his own self-enamored eye.

I have Come to Initiate a truly Divine New Age of Real-God-Man, by Means of My forever Divine "Emergence" here and every where in the Cosmic domain.

I have Come to Turn mankind (and even all beings, and even the Cosmic All Itself) to My own Divine Person, the "Bright" Reality and Truth and Self-Condition and Source-Condition of all and All.

I Have Come to Found (and, altogether, to Make Possible) a New (and Truly "Bright") Age of mankind, an Age That will not begin on the basis of the seeking mummery of ego-bondage, but an Age in Which mankind will apply itself, apart from all dilemma and all seeking, to the Inherently Harmonious Event of Real existence (in the Always Already present-time "Bright" Divine Reality That Is the One and Only Reality Itself).

I Am Certain That This "Bright" New Truly Human Age, Initiated by My Divine "Emergence" here, and generated via the Seed That Is the "Bright" New Human Order of My true devotees, must Arise with Great Force in the world in the present historical "dark" epoch (or "late-time"). This by-Me-Initiated "Bright" New Age of Real-God-Man must replace (or turn about) the otherwise present-time (and proceeding) trend and destiny of mankind, or else, due to the causes made by the casually destructive force of ego-bound sub-humanity, this mankind-world will suffer like a mind in nightmares (possessed by terrible self-inflicted images, and likewise put to awful adventures, made by fear, sorrow, anger, life-depression, and loveless-ness). And, if This "Bright" New Age does not soon begin, with Great Force, it may even come about (in this Klik-Klak[40] mummery of ego-minded Man) that the physical human world itself may, by its own hand, suffer the terrible and immensely bewildering humiliation of early dissolution.

Therefore, just As I Moved and Obliged My own ordi-nary body-mind to Conform Most Perfectly to Me, I will Shout and Move, with ego-Overwhelming Force (of Love-Instruction and Divinely "Emerging" Blessing-Power), to Move and Oblige "Narcissus" (as every one, and all) to Stand Up from the ego's filth and pond, and, In That love-Stand of the heart's recognition-response to Me, to Con-sent to My Love-Bliss, and to <u>Be</u> Love-Bliss, In <u>Me</u>, the "Bright" Real-God-Man of the Now and New "Emerging" Age.

And I Will <u>Not</u> Be Denied My all-and-All-Liberating Victory in the heart (and in all the world) of Man!

Notes to the Text of

ELEUTHERIOS
(THE <u>ONLY</u> TRUTH THAT SETS THE HEART FREE)

Part One

1. "Eleutherios" (Greek for "Liberator") is a title by which Zeus was venerated as the supreme deity in the Spiritual esotericism of ancient Greece. The Designation "Eleutherios" indicates the Divine Function of Avatar Adi Da as the Incarnation of the Divine Person, "Whose Inherently Perfect Self-'Brightness' Liberates all conditionally Manifested beings, Freely, Liberally, Gracefully, and Without Ceasing".

2. The ego-"I" is the fundamental self-contraction, or the sense of separate and separative existence.

3. "Difference" is the epitome of the egoic presumption of separateness—in contrast with the Realization of Oneness, or Non-"Difference", that is native to Spiritual and Transcendental Divine Self-Consciousness.

4. The term "radical" derives from the Latin "radix", meaning "root", and thus it principally means "irreducible", "fundamental", or "relating to the origin". In *The Dawn Horse Testament Of The Ruchira Avatar, The "Testament Of Secrets" Of The Divine World-Teacher, Ruchira Avatar Adi Da Samraj*, Avatar Adi Da defines "Radical" as "Gone To The Root, Core, Source, or Origin". Because Adi Da Samraj uses "radical" in this literal sense, it appears in quotation marks in His Wisdom-Teaching, in order to distinguish His usage from the common reference to an extreme (often political) view.

5. Avatar Adi Da uses "Self-Existing and Self-Radiant" to indicate the two fundamental aspects of the One Divine Person—Existence (or Being, or Consciousness) Itself, and Radiance (or Energy, or Light) Itself.

6. The technical term "consider" or "consideration" in Avatar Adi Da's Wisdom-Teaching means a process of one-pointed but ultimately thoughtless concentration and exhaustive contemplation of something until its ultimate obviousness is clear. As engaged in the Way of Adidam, "consideration" is not merely an intellectual investigation. It is the participatory investment of one's whole being. If one "considers" something fully in the context of one's practice of feeling-Contemplation of Avatar Adi Da Samraj, this concentration results "in

both the highest intuition and the most practical grasp of the Lawful and Divine necessities of human existence".

7. Avatar Adi Da Affirms that there is a Divine Self-Domain that is the Perfectly Subjective Condition of the conditional worlds. It is not "elsewhere", not an objective "place" (like a subtle "heaven" or mythical "paradise"), but It is the always present, Transcendental, Inherently Spiritual, Divine Source-Condition of every conditionally manifested being and thing. Avatar Adi Da Reveals that the Divine Self-Domain is not other than the Divine Heart Itself, Who He <u>Is</u>. To Realize the seventh stage of life (by the Grace of Avatar Adi Da Samraj) is to Awaken to the Divine Self-Domain.

8. By the word "Bright" (and its variations, such as "Brightness"), Avatar Adi Da refers to the eternally, infinitely, and inherently Self-Radiant Divine Being, the Being of Indivisible and Indestructible Light. As Adi Da Writes in His Spiritual Autobiography, *The Knee Of Listening, The Seventeen Companions Of The True Dawn Horse, Book Four: The Early-Life Ordeal and The "Radical" Spiritual Realization Of The Ruchira Avatar*:

> . . . *from my earliest experience of life I have Enjoyed a Condition that, as a child, I called the "Bright".*
>
> *I have always known desire, not merely for extreme pleasures of the senses and the mind, but for the highest Enjoyment of Spiritual Power and Mobility. But I have not been seated in desire, and desire has only been a play that I have grown to understand and enjoy without conflict. I have always been Seated in the "Bright".*
>
> *Even as a baby I remember only crawling around inquisitively with a boundless Feeling of Joy, Light, and Freedom in the middle of my head that was bathed in Energy moving unobstructed in a Circle, down from above, all the way down, then up, all the way up, and around again, and always Shining from my heart. It was an Expanding Sphere of Joy from the heart. And I was a Radiant Form, the Source of Energy, Love-Bliss, and Light in the midst of a world that is entirely Energy, Love-Bliss, and Light. I was the Power of Reality, a direct Enjoyment and Communication of the One Reality. I was the Heart Itself, Who Lightens the mind and all things. I was the same as every one and every thing, except it became clear that others were apparently unaware of the "Thing" Itself.*
>
> *Even as a little child I recognized It and Knew It, and my life was not a matter of anything else. That Awareness, that Conscious Enjoyment, that Self-Existing and Self-Radiant Space of Infinitely and inherently Free Being, that Shine of inherent Joy Standing in the heart and Expanding from the heart, is the "Bright". And It is the entire Source of True Humor. It is Reality. It is not separate from anything.*

9. Avatar Adi Da Samraj spontaneously Gave the Name "Adidam" in January 1996. This primary Name for the Way He has Revealed and Given is simply His own Principal Name ("Adi Da") with the addition of "m" at the end. When He first Gave this Name, Adi Da Samraj pointed out that the final "m" adds a mantric force, evoking the effect of the primal Sanskrit syllable "Om". (For Avatar Adi Da's Revelation of the most profound esoteric significance of "Om" as the Divine Sound of His own Very Being, see *He-and-She Is Me, The Seventeen Companions Of The True Dawn Horse, Book Seven: The Indivisibility Of Consciousness and Light In The Divine Body Of The Ruchira Avatar*.) Simultaneously, the final "m" suggests the English word "Am" (expressing "I Am"), such that the Name "Adidam" also evokes Avatar Adi Da's Primal Self-Confession, "I Am Adi Da", or, more simply, "I Am Da" (or "Aham Da Asmi").

10. "Avatar" (from Sanskrit "avatara") is a traditional term for the Divine Incarnation. It literally means "One who is descended, or 'crossed down' (from, and as, the Divine)". In Sanskrit, "Ruchira" means "bright, radiant, effulgent". Thus, the Reference "Ruchira Avatar" indicates that Avatar Adi Da Samraj is the "Bright" (or Radiant) Descent of the Divine Reality Itself (or the Divine Truth Itself, Which Is the Only Real God) into the conditional worlds, Appearing here in bodily (human) Form.

11. The Name "Da", combined with the Reference "Avatar", fully acknowledges Avatar Adi Da Samraj as the original, first, and complete Descent of the Very Divine Person, Who is Named "Da". Through the Mystery of Avatar Adi Da's human Birth, He has Incarnated not only in this world but in every world, at every level of the Cosmic domain, as the Eternal Giver of Help and Grace and Divine Freedom to all beings, now and forever hereafter.

12. The Name "Love-Ananda" combines both English ("Love") and Sanskrit ("Ananda", meaning "Bliss"), thus bridging the West and the East, and communicating Avatar Adi Da's Function as the Divine World-Teacher. The combination of "Love" and "Ananda" means "the Divine Love-Bliss". The Name "Love-Ananda" was given to Avatar Adi Da by His principal human Spiritual Master, Swami Muktananda, who spontaneously conferred it upon Avatar Adi Da in 1969. However, Avatar Adi Da did not use the Name "Love-Ananda" until April 1986, after the Great Event that Initiated His Divine "Emergence". As the Love-Ananda Avatar, Avatar Adi Da is the Very Incarnation of the Divine Love-Bliss.

13. "The 'late-time'" is a phrase that Avatar Adi Da uses to Describe the present era, in which doubt of God (and of anything at all beyond mortal existence) is more and more pervading the entire world, and in which the separate and separative ego-"I", which is the root of all suffering and conflict, is regarded to be the ultimate principle of life.

14. Avatar Adi Da uses the phrase "Most Perfect(ly)" in the sense of "Absolutely Perfect(ly)". Similarly, the phrase "Most Ultimate(ly)" is equivalent to "Absolutely Ultimate(ly)". "Most Perfect(ly)" and "Most Ultimate(ly)" are always references to the seventh (or Divinely Enlightened) stage of life. (See note 21.)

15. The "Perfect Practice" is Avatar Adi Da's technical term for the discipline of the sixth stage of life and the seventh stage of life in the Way of Adidam.

Devotees who have mastered (and, thus, transcended) the point of view of the body-mind by fulfilling the preparatory processes of the Way of Adidam may, by Avatar Adi Da's Grace, be Awakened to practice in the Domain of Consciousness Itself, in the sixth and seventh (or ultimate) stages of life.

16. Feeling-Contemplation is Avatar Adi Da's term for the essential devotional and meditative practice that all practitioners of the Way of Adidam engage at all times in relationship to His bodily (human) Form, His Spiritual (and Always Blessing) Presence, and His Very (and Inherently Perfect) State. Feeling-Contemplation of Adi Da Samraj is Awakened by Grace through Darshan, or feeling-sighting, of His Form, Presence, and State. It is then to be practiced under all conditions, and as the basis and epitome of all other practices in the Way of Adidam.

17. Avatar Adi Da uses the terms "Spiritual", "Transcendental", and "Divine" in reference to different dimensions of Reality that are Realized progressively in the Way of Adidam. "Spiritual" refers to the reception of the Spirit-Force (in the "basic" and "advanced" contexts of the fourth stage of life and in the context of the fifth stage of life); "Transcendental" refers to the Realization of Consciousness Itself as separate from the world (in the context of the sixth stage of life); and "Divine" refers to the Most Perfect Realization of Consciousness Itself as utterly Non-separate from the world (in the context of the seventh stage of life). (For Avatar Adi Da's fully extended discussion of the stages of life, see *The Seven Stages Of Life*.)

18. "Listening" is Avatar Adi Da's term for the orientation, disposition, and beginning practice of the Way of Adidam. A listening devotee

"listens" to Avatar Adi Da Samraj by "considering" His Teaching Argument and His Leelas, and by practicing feeling-Contemplation of Him (primarily of His bodily human Form). In the total (or full and complete) practice of the Way of Adidam, effective listening is the necessary prerequisite for true hearing and true seeing.

19. Avatar Adi Da describes His Divine Being on three levels:

This flesh body, this bodily (human) Sign, is My Form, in the sense that it is My Murti, or a kind of Reflection, or Representation, of Me. It is, therefore, a Means for contacting My Spiritual (and Always Blessing) Presence, and, ultimately, My Very (and Inherently Perfect) State.

My Spiritual (and Always Blessing) Presence is Self-Existing and Self-Radiant. It Functions in time and space, and It is also Prior to all time and space. . . .

My Very (and Inherently Perfect) State is always and only utterly Prior to time and space. Therefore, I, As I Am (Ultimately), have no "Function" in time and space. There is no time and space in My Very (and Inherently Perfect) State.

20. "Hearing" is a technical term used by Avatar Adi Da to Describe most fundamental understanding of the act of egoity (or self-contraction). Hearing is the unique capability to directly transcend the self-contraction, such that, simultaneous with that transcendence, there is the intuitive awakening to the Revelation of the Divine Person and Self-Condition. The capability of true hearing can only be Granted by Avatar Adi Da's Grace, to His fully practicing devotee who has effectively completed the process of listening. Only on the basis of such hearing can Spiritually Awakened practice of the Way of Adidam truly (or with full responsibility) begin.

I Am Heard When My Listening Devotee Has Truly (and Thoroughly) Observed the ego-"I" and Understood it (Directly, In the moments Of self-Observation, and Most Fundamentally, or In its Totality).

I Am Heard When the ego-"I" Is Altogether (and Thoroughly) Observed and (Most Fundamentally) Understood, Both In The Tendency To Dissociate and In The Tendency To Become Attached (or To Cling By Wanting Need, or To Identify With others, and things, and circumstances egoically, and Thus To Dramatize The Seeker, Bereft Of Basic Equanimity, Wholeness, and The Free Capability For Simple Relatedness).

I Am Heard When the ego-"I" Is Thoroughly (and Most Fundamentally) Understood To Be Contraction-Only, An Un-Necessary and Destructive Motive and Design, Un-Naturally and Chronically Added

*To Cosmic Nature and To all relations, and An Imaginary Heart-Disease
(Made To Seem Real, By Heart-Reaction).*

*I Am Heard When This Most Fundamental Understanding Of
The Habit Of "Narcissus" Becomes The Directly Obvious Realization
Of The Heart, Radiating Beyond Its Own (Apparent) Contraction.*

*I Am Heard When The Beginning Is Full, and The Beginning Is
Full (and Ended) When Every Gesture Of self-Contraction (In The
Context Of The First Three Stages Of Life, and Relative To Each and
All Of The Principal Faculties, Of body, emotion, mind, and breath) Is
(As A Rather Consistently Applied and humanly Effective Discipline)
Observed (By Natural feeling-perception), Tacitly (and Most Funda-
mentally) Understood, and Really (Directly and Effectively) Felt
Beyond (In The Prior Feeling Of Unqualified Relatedness).* (The Dawn
Horse Testament Of The Ruchira Avatar, chapter nineteen)

21. Avatar Adi Da has Revealed the underlying structure of human
growth in seven stages.

The first three stages of life develop, respectively, the physical,
emotional, and mental/volitional functions of the body-mind. The
first stage begins at birth and continues for approximately five to
seven years; the second stage follows, continuing until approximately
the age of twelve to fourteen; and the third stage is optimally complete by the early twenties. In the case of virtually all individuals,
however, failed adaptation in the earlier stages of life means that
maturity in the third stage of life takes much longer to attain, and it is
usually never fulfilled, with the result that the ensuing stages of Spiritual development do not even begin.

In the Way of Adidam, however, growth in the first three stages
of life unfolds in the Spiritual Company of Avatar Adi Da and is based
in the practice of feeling-Contemplation of His bodily (human) Form
and in devotion, service, and self-discipline in relation to His bodily
(human) Form. By the Grace of this relationship to Avatar Adi Da, the
first three (or foundation) stages of life are lived and fulfilled in a self-
transcending devotional disposition, or (as He Describes it) "in the
'original' or beginner's devotional context of the fourth stage of life".

The fourth stage of life is the transitional stage between the
gross, bodily-based point of view of the first three stages of life and
the subtle, psychic point of view of the fifth stage of life. The fourth
stage of life is the stage of Spiritual devotion, or surrender of separate
self, in which the gross functions of the being are submitted to the
higher psychic, or subtle, functions of the being, and, through these
psychic functions, to the Divine. In the fourth stage of life, the gross,
or bodily-based, personality of the first three stages of life is purified
through reception of the Spiritual Force ("Holy Spirit", or "Shakti") of

the Divine Reality, Which prepares the being to out-grow the bodily-based point of view.

In the Way of Adidam, as the orientation of the fourth stage of life matures, heart-felt surrender to the bodily (human) Form of Avatar Adi Da deepens by Grace, drawing His devotee into Love-Communion with His All-Pervading Spiritual Presence. Growth in the "basic" context of the fourth stage of life in the Way of Adidam is also characterized by a Baptizing Current of Spirit-Energy that is at first felt to flow down the front of the body from above the head to the bodily base.

The Descent of Avatar Adi Da's Spirit-Baptism releases obstructions predominantly in the waking, or frontal, personality. This frontal Yoga purifies His devotee and infuses him or her with His Spirit-Power. Avatar Adi Da's devotee is awakened to profound love of and devotional intimacy with Him.

If the transition to the sixth stage of life is not otherwise made at maturity in the "basic" context of the fourth stage of life, the Spirit-Current is felt to turn about at the bodily base and ascend to the brain core, and the fourth stage of life matures to its "advanced" context, which involves the ascent of Avatar Adi Da's Spiritual Blessing and purifies the spinal line of the body-mind.

In the fifth stage of life, attention is concentrated in the subtle, or psychic, levels of awareness in ascent. The Spirit-Current is felt to penetrate the brain core and rise toward the Matrix of Light and Love-Bliss infinitely above the crown of the head, possibly culminating in the temporary experience of fifth stage conditional Nirvikalpa Samadhi, or "formless ecstasy". In the Way of Adidam, most practitioners will not need to practice in the context of the fifth stage of life, but will rather be Awakened, by Adi Da's Grace, from maturity in the fourth stage of life to the Witness-Position of Consciousness (in the context of the sixth stage of life).

In the traditional development of the sixth stage of life, attention is inverted upon the essential self and the Perfectly Subjective Position of Consciousness, to the exclusion of conditional phenomena. In the Way of Adidam, however, the deliberate intention to invert attention for the sake of Realizing Transcendental Consciousness does not characterize the sixth stage of life, which instead begins when the Witness-Position of Consciousness spontaneously Awakens and becomes stable.

In the course of the sixth stage of life, the mechanism of attention, which is the root-action of egoity (felt as separation, self-contraction, or the feeling of relatedness), gradually subsides. In the fullest context of the sixth stage of life, the knot of attention dissolves and all sense of relatedness yields to the Blissful and undifferentiated Feeling of

Being. The characteristic Samadhi of the sixth stage of life is Jnana Samadhi, the temporary and exclusive Realization of the Transcendental Self, or Consciousness Itself.

The transition from the sixth stage of life to the seventh stage Realization of Absolute Non-Separateness is the unique Revelation of Avatar Adi Da. Various traditions and individuals previous to Adi Da's Revelation have had sixth stage intuitions or premonitions of the Most Perfect seventh stage Realization, but no one previous to Avatar Adi Da has Realized the seventh stage of life.

The seventh stage Realization is the Gift of Avatar Adi Da to His devotees, Awakened only in the context of the Way of Adidam that He has Revealed and Given. The seventh stage of life begins when His devotee Awakens, by His Grace, from the exclusive Realization of Consciousness to Most Perfect and permanent Identification with Consciousness Itself, Avatar Adi Da's Very (and Inherently Perfect) State. This is Divine Self-Realization, or Divine Enlightenment, the perpetual Samadhi of "Open Eyes" (seventh stage Sahaj Samadhi), in which all "things" are Divinely Recognized without "difference" as merely apparent modifications of the One Self-Existing and Self-Radiant Divine Consciousness. In the course of the seventh stage of life, there may be spontaneous incidents in which psycho-physical states and phenomena do not appear to the notice, being Outshined by the "Bright" Radiance of Consciousness Itself. This Samadhi, which is the ultimate Realization of Divine Existence, culminates in Divine Translation, or the permanent Outshining of all apparent conditions in the Inherently Perfect Radiance and Love-Bliss of the Divine Self-Condition.

In the context of practice of the Way of Adidam, the seven stages of life as Revealed by Avatar Adi Da are not a version of the traditional "ladder" of Spiritual attainment. These stages and their characteristic signs arise naturally in the course of practice for a fully practicing devotee in the Way of Adidam, but the practice itself is oriented to the <u>transcending</u> of the first six stages of life, in the seventh stage Disposition of Inherently Liberated Happiness, Granted by Grace in the Love-Blissful Spiritual Company of Avatar Adi Da.

22. When, in the practice of the Way of Adidam, hearing (or most fundamental self-understanding) is steadily exercised in meditation and in life, the native feeling of the heart ceases to be chronically constricted by self-contraction. The heart then begins to Radiate as love in response to the Spiritual (and Always Blessing) Presence of Avatar Adi Da.

This emotional and Spiritual response of the whole being is what Avatar Da calls "seeing". Seeing is emotional conversion from the reactive emotions that characterize egoic self-obsession, to the open-hearted, Radiant Happiness that characterizes God-Love and Spiritual devotion to Avatar Adi Da. This true and stable emotional conversion coincides with true and stable receptivity to Avatar Adi Da's Spiritual Transmission, and both of these are prerequisites to further Spiritual advancement in the Way of Adidam.

Seeing Is self-Transcending Participation In Wbat *(and* Wbo*)* Is. *Seeing Is Love. Seeing, or Love, Is Able (By My Grace) To "Locate", Recognize, and Feel My All-Pervading Spiritual Radiance (and My Spirit-Identity,* As *The Divine Person, or The "Bright" and Only One* Wbo Is*). Therefore, Seeing Is Heart-Felt and Whole bodily Identification Of The Love-Bliss-Presence and Person (or Mere Being) Of The Divine. Seeing Is Spiritually Activated Conversion Of attention, emotion, and the Total psycho-physical personality From self-Contraction To The Spiritual Form (or Tangible Spiritual Presence) Of Real God (or The Necessarily Divine Reality and Truth, Itself), and This Via My Spirit-Baptism (or Divine and Inherently Perfect Hridaya-Shaktipat, or Divine and Inherently Perfect Heart-Awakening, and The Subsequent Apparent Descent and Circulation Of The Divine Spirit-Force Into and Through and, Ultimately, Beyond the body-mind Of My Progressively Awakening Devotee). Seeing Is Spontaneous (or Heart-Moved) Devotional Sacrifice Of the self-Contraction. Seeing Is The "Radical" (or Directly self-Transcending) Reorientation Of conditional Existence To The Transcendental, Inherently Spiritual, and Inherently Perfect Divine Self-Condition (and Source-Condition) In Whom (or In Which) conditional self and conditional worlds Apparently arise and Always Already Inhere.*

Seeing, Like Hearing, Is A "Radical" (or "Gone To The Root, Core, Source, or Origin") Capability That Can and Should Be Exercised moment to moment. When There Is (In any moment) Real Seeing Of Me, There Is The Capability To Contact Me Spiritually and Enter Into Communion With Me Spiritually. When You Have Awakened (By My Grace) To See Me Truly, Then The Act (and Sadhana) Of Contacting Me Spiritually Does Not, In every *moment Of Its Exercise, Require That You Come Into The Physical Sphere Of My Bodily (Human) Form (or, After The Physical Lifetime Of My Bodily Human Form, Into The physical Sphere Of My "Living Murti") or That You Enter Into a place Spiritually Empowered By Me. My Devotee Who Sees Me Is (In The General Course Of moment to moment Practice Of Devotion To Me) Capable Of Contacting Me Spiritually In any circumstance, By Using The "Radical" Virtue Of Hearing and Seeing To Go Beyond The self-Contracting Tendency.*

Seeing Is Simply Attraction To Me, and Feeling Me, As My Spiritual (and Always Blessing) Presence, and This Most Fundamentally, At The Root, Core, Source, or Origin Of The Emergence Of My Presence "here" (At and In Front Of The Heart, or At and In The Root-Context Of the body-mind, or At and In The Source-Position, and, Ultimately, As The Source-Condition, Of conditional, or psycho-physical, Existence Itself).

Seeing Is Knowing Me As My Spiritual (and Always Blessing) Presence, Just As Tangibly, and With The Same Degree Of Clarity, As You Would Differentiate The Physical Appearance Of My Bodily (Human) Form From the physical appearance of the bodily (human) form of any other.

To See Me Is A Clear and "Radical" Knowledge Of Me, About Which There Is No Doubt. To See Me Is A Sudden, Tacit Awareness, Like Walking Into a "thicker" air or atmosphere, or Suddenly Feeling a breeze, or Jumping Into water and Noticing The Difference In Density Between the air and the water. This Tangible Feeling Of Me Is (In any particular moment) Not Necessarily (Otherwise) Associated With effects in the body-mind . . . , but It Is, Nevertheless, Felt At The Heart and Even All Over the body.

Seeing Is One-Pointedness In The "Radical" Conscious Process Of Heart-Devotion To Me. (The Dawn Horse Testament Of The Ruchira Avatar, chapter twenty)

For Avatar Adi Da's fundamental Instruction relative to listening, hearing, and seeing, see chapters nineteen and twenty of *The Dawn Horse Testament Of The Ruchira Avatar*, or chapters twenty-one through twenty-three and chapters twenty-four through twenty-eight of *The Heart Of The Dawn Horse Testament Of The Ruchira Avatar, The Seventeen Companions Of The True Dawn Horse, Book Twelve: The Epitome Of The "Testament Of Secrets" Of The Divine World-Teacher, Ruchira Avatar Adi Da Samraj.*

23. Conventionally, "self-possessed" means possessed <u>of</u> oneself—or in full control (calmness, or composure) of one's feelings, impulses, habits, and actions. Avatar Adi Da uses the term to indicate the state of being possessed <u>by</u> one's egoic self, or controlled by chronically self-referring (or egoic) tendencies of attention, feeling, thought, desire, and action.

24. One of the four phases of the seventh stage process. (See note 21.)

25. Avatar Adi Da uses "Outshining" as a synonym for "Divine Translation", to refer to the final Demonstration of the four-phase process of the seventh, or Divinely Enlightened, stage of life in the Way of Adidam. In the Great Event of Outshining, or Divine Translation, body, mind, and world are no longer noticed—not because the Divine Consciousness has withdrawn or dissociated from conditionally

manifested phenomena, but because the Divine Recognition of all arising phenomena as modifications of the Divine Self has become so intense that the "Bright" Radiance of Consciousness now Outshines all such phenomena.

For Avatar Adi Da's Instruction relative to the four phases of the seventh stage of life, see *The Seven Stages Of Life*.

26. The Feeling of Being is the uncaused (or Self-Existing), Self-Radiant, and unqualified feeling-intuition of the Transcendental, Inherently Spiritual, and Divine Self. This absolute Feeling does not merely accompany or express the Realization of the Heart Itself, but It is Identical to that Realization. To feel—or, really, to Be—the Feeling of Being is to enjoy the Love-Bliss of Absolute Consciousness, Which, when Most Perfectly Realized, cannot be prevented or even diminished either by the events of life or by death.

27. When Consciousness is free of identification with the body-mind, it takes up its natural "position" as the Conscious Witness of all that arises to and in and as the body-mind.

In the Way of Adidam, the stable Realization of the Witness-Position is associated with, or demonstrated via, the effortless surrender (or relaxation) of all the forms of seeking and all the motives of attention that characterize the first five stages of life. However, identification with the Witness-Position is not final (or Most Perfect) Realization of the Divine Self. Rather, it is the first of the three stages of the "Perfect Practice" in the Way of Adidam, which Practice, in due course, Realizes, by Avatar Adi Da's Liberating Grace, complete and irreversible and utterly Love-Blissful Identification with Consciousness Itself.

28. In Avatar Adi Da's Teaching-Revelation, "Narcissus" is a key symbol of the un-Enlightened individual as a self-obsessed seeker, enamored of his or her own self-image and egoic self-consciousness. In *The Knee Of Listening*, Adi Da Samraj Describes the significance of the archetype of Narcissus:

He is the ancient one visible in the Greek "myth", who was the universally adored child of the gods, who rejected the loved-one and every form of love and relationship, who was finally condemned to the contemplation of his own image, until, as a result of his own act and obstinacy, he suffered the fate of eternal separateness and died in infinite solitude.

29. In the foundation stages of practice in the Way of Adidam, the basic (or gross) manifestation of the avoidance of relationship is understood and released when Avatar Adi Da's devotee hears Him (or comes to point of most fundamental self-understanding), thereby

regaining the free capability for simple relatedness, or living on the basis of the feeling of relatedness rather than the avoidance of relationship. But the feeling of relatedness is not Ultimate Realization, because it is still founded in the presumption of a "difference" between "I" and "other". Only in the ultimate stages of life in the Way of Adidam is the feeling of relatedness itself fully understood as the root-act of attention and, ultimately, transcended in the Feeling of Being. Adi Da Samraj points out that the feeling of relatedness is, at root, the <u>avoidance</u> of relationship in relation to <u>all</u> others and things, or the root-activity of separation, separateness, and separativeness that <u>is</u> the ego.

30. "Open Eyes" is Avatar Adi Da's technical synonym for the Realization of seventh stage Sahaj Samadhi, or unqualified Divine Self-Realization. The phrase graphically describes the non-exclusive, non-inward, Native State of the Divine Self-Realizer, Who is Identified Unconditionally with the Divine Self-Reality, while also allowing whatever arises to appear in the Divine Consciousness (and spontaneously Recognizing everything that arises as merely an unnecessary modification of That One). The Transcendental Self is intuited in the mature phases of the sixth stage of life, but It can be Realized at that stage only by the intentional exclusion of conditional phenomena. In "Open Eyes", that impulse to exclusion disappears, when the Eyes of the Heart Open and Most Perfect Realization of the Spiritual, Transcendental, and Divine Self in the seventh stage of life becomes permanent and incorruptible by any phenomenal events.

31. In the context of Divine Enlightenment in the seventh stage of life in the Way of Adidam, the Spiritual process continues. Avatar Adi Da has uniquely Revealed the four phases of the seventh stage process: Divine Transfiguration, Divine Transformation, Divine Indifference, and Divine Translation.

In the phase of Divine Transfiguration, the devotee-Realizer's body-mind is Infused by Avatar Adi Da's Love-Bliss, and he or she Radiantly Demonstrates active Love, spontaneously Blessing all the relations of the body-mind.

In the following phase of Divine Transformation, the subtle (or psychic) dimension of the body-mind is fully Illumined, which may result in Divine Powers of healing, longevity, and the ability to release obstacles from the world and from the lives of others.

Divine Translation is the most ultimate "Event" of the entire process of Divine Awakening. Avatar Adi Da Describes Divine Translation as the Outshining of all noticing of objective conditions, through the infinitely magnified Force of Consciousness Itself. Divine Translation is the Outshining of all destinies, wherein there is no return to the conditional realms.

For Avatar Adi Da's Instruction relative to the four phases of the seventh stage of life, see *The Seven Stages Of Life*.

32. In Sanskrit, "Ruchira" means "bright", or "brightness", and "Ati" means "beyond", or "all-surpassing". "Ati-Ruchira Yoga", or "the Yoga of the All-Outshining 'Brightness'", is Avatar Adi Da's term for "Practice" in the context the four phases of the seventh stage of life in the Way of Adidam.

33. Avatar Adi Da Samraj is the "Avataric Incarnation", or the Divinely Descended Embodiment, of the Divine Person. The reference "Avataric Incarnation" indicates that Avatar Adi Da Samraj fulfills both the traditional expectation of the East—that the True God-Man is an Avatar, or an utterly Divine "Descent" of Real God in conditionally manifested form—and the traditional expectations of the West—that the True God-Man is an Incarnation, or an utterly human Embodiment of Real God.

For Avatar Adi Da's discussion of the "Avatar" and "Incarnation" traditions, and of His unique and all-Completing Role as the "Avataric Incarnation" of the Divine Person, see "'Avatar' and 'Incarnation': The Complementary God-Man Traditions of East and West", in *The Truly Human New World-Culture Of <u>Unbroken</u> Real-God-Man, The Seventeen Companions Of The True Dawn Horse, Book Two: The <u>Eastern</u> Versus The <u>Western</u> Traditional Cultures Of Mankind, and The Unique New <u>Non-Dual</u> Culture Of The True World-Religion Of Adidam*).

34. Avadhoot is a traditional term for one who has "shaken off" or "passed beyond" all worldly attachments and cares, including all motives of detachment (or conventional and other-worldly renunciation), all conventional notions of life and religion, and all seeking for "answers" or "solutions" in the form of conditional experience or conditional knowledge. Therefore, "'Crazy' Avadhoot", in reference to Avatar Adi Da, indicates His Inherently Perfect Freedom as the One Who Knows His Identity As the Divine Person and Who, thus, Always Already Stands Free of the binding and deluding power of conditional existence.

35. On January 11, 1986, Avatar Adi Da passed through a profound Yogic Swoon, which He later described as the initial Event of His Divine "Emergence". Avatar Adi Da's Divine "Emergence" is an ongoing Process in which His bodily (human) Form has been (and is ever more profoundly and potently being) conformed to Himself, the Very Divine Person, such that His bodily (human) Form is now (and forever hereafter) an utterly Unobstructed Sign and Agent of His own Divine Being.

For Avatar Adi Da's Revelation of the significance of His Divine "Emergence", see *The Dawn Horse Testament Of The Ruchira Avatar* or *The Heart Of The Dawn Horse Testament Of The Ruchira Avatar*, Part One, "The True Dawn Horse <u>Is</u> The <u>Only</u> Way To Me", section III.

Part Two

36. Avatar Adi Da Samraj uses the term "advanced" to Describe the fourth stage of life (in its "basic" and "advanced" contexts) and the fifth stage of life in the Way of Adidam. He reserves the term "ultimate" to Describe the sixth and seventh stages of life in the Way of Adidam.

Part Three

37. Avatar Adi Da uses the terms "bond" and "bonding", when lower-cased, to refer to the process by which the egoic individual (already presuming separateness, and, therefore, bondage to the separate self) attaches itself karmically to the world of others and things through the constant search for self-fulfillment. In contrast, when He capitalizes the term "Bond" (or "Bonding"), Avatar Adi Da is making reference to the process of His devotee's devotional "Bonding" to Him, which process is the Great Means for transcending all forms of limited, or karmic, "bonding".

Part Four

38. "Samsara" (or "samsaric") is a classical Buddhist and Hindu term for all conditional worlds and states, or the realm of birth and change and death. It connotes the suffering and limitations experienced in those limited worlds.

39. For a discussion of the Body of Avatar Adi Da's Divine Wisdom-Teaching, please see pp. 29-35.

Epilogue

40. Avatar Adi Da has coined the term "Klik-Klak" as a name for the conditional reality. This name indicates (even by means of the sound of the two syllables) that the conditional reality is a heartless perpetual-motion machine of incessant change.

For Avatar Adi Da's extended Instruction relative to Klik-Klak, see "Klik-Klak and My Laughing Mama Form", in *The Mummery— The Seventeen Companions Of The True Dawn Horse, Book Six: A Parable About Finding The Way To My House.*

What You Can Do Next

Contact one of our centers.

■ Sign up for our preliminary course, "The <u>Only</u> Truth That Sets The Heart Free". This course will prepare you to become a fully practicing devotee of Avatar Adi Da Samraj.

■ Or sign up for any of our other classes, seminars, events, or retreats, or for a study course available by correspondence:

AMERICAS
12040 North Seigler Road
Middletown, CA 95461
(800) 524-4941
(707) 928-4936

PACIFIC-ASIA
12 Seibel Road
Henderson
Auckland 1008
New Zealand
64-9-838-9114

AUSTRALIA
P.O. Box 460
Roseville, NSW 2069
Australia
61-2-9416-7951

EUROPE-AFRICA
Annendaalderweg 10
6105 AT Maria Hoop
The Netherlands
31 (0)20 468 1442

THE UNITED KINGDOM
London, England
0181-7317550

E-MAIL: correspondence@adidam.org

Read these books by and about the Divine World-Teacher, Ruchira Avatar Adi Da Samraj:

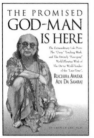

■ *The Promised God-Man Is Here*

The Extraordinary Life-Story, The "Crazy" Teaching-Work, and The Divinely "Emerging" World-Blessing Work Of The Divine World-Teacher Of The "Late-Time", Ruchira Avatar Adi Da Samraj, by Carolyn Lee, Ph.D.—the profound, heart-rending, humorous, miraculous, wild—and true—story of the Divine Person Alive in human Form. Essential reading as background for the study of Avatar Adi Da's books.

■ *See My Brightness Face to Face*

A Celebration of the Ruchira Avatar, Adi Da Samraj, and the First Twenty-Five Years of His Divine Revelation Work—a magnificent year-by-year pictorial celebration of Ruchira Avatar Adi Da's Divine Work with His devotees, from 1972-1997. Includes a wealth of selections from His Talks and Writings, numerous Stories of His Divine Work told by His devotees, and over 100 color photographs.

■ *Aham Da Asmi (Beloved, I <u>Am</u> Da)*

The Five Books Of The Heart Of The Adidam Revelation, Book One: The "Late-Time" Avataric Revelation Of The True and Spiritual Divine Person (The egoless Personal Presence Of Reality and Truth, Which <u>Is</u> The Only <u>Real</u> God)

This Ecstatic Scripture, the first of His twenty-three "Source-Texts", contains Ruchira Avatar Adi Da's magnificent Confession of His Identity as the Very Divine Person and Source-Condition of all and All.

After reading *Aham Da Asmi*, continue your reading with the remaining books of *The Five Books Of The Heart Of The Adidam Revelation* (the *Ruchira Avatara Gita*, the *Da Love-Ananda Gita*, and *Hridaya Rosary*). Then you will be ready to go on to *The Seventeen Companions Of The True Dawn Horse* (see pp. 243-47). These and other books by and about Ruchira Avatar Adi Da Samraj can be ordered directly from the Dawn Horse Press by calling:

(800) 524-4941 (from within North America)
(707) 928-4936 (from outside North America)

or by writing to:

The Dawn Horse Press
12040 North Seigler Road
Middletown, CA 95461

Or you can order these, or any of the other products distributed by the Dawn Horse Press, by visiting the Dawn Horse Press on-line at: **http://dhp.adidam.org**.

Visit our website:
http://www.adidam.org.

Our award-winning website contains a wealth of photographs of Ruchira Avatar Adi Da Samraj, audio-clips of Him Speaking, excerpts from His Writings, and recent Stories of His world-Blessing Work. The website also has a full listing of Adidam regional centers worldwide.

For a full description of all the forms of involvement in the Way of Adidam, see "Surely Come to Me" on pp. 219-39.

RUCHIRA AVATAR ADI DA SAMRAJ
Adidam Samrajashram (Naitauba), Fiji, 1997

"Surely Come to Me"

An Invitation to the Way of Adidam

I __Am__ The Divine Heart-Master. I Take My Stand In The Heart Of My Devotee. Have You Realized The Heart, Who __Is__ The Mystery Of You and Me?

How Could I Deny Heart-Vision To My Loved-One?

How Could I Delay The Course Of My Beloved?

Like An Intimate Family Servant, I Dearly Serve My Devotee.

Like A Wealthy Friend, I Freely Give To My Devotee.

Like A Mad Priest, I Even Worship My Devotee, With Love Itself.

Like An Innocent Boy At First Love, I Would Awaken My Devotee In Radiant Chambers.

Where The Wound Of Love Churns and Never Heals, I Wait, Longing To Celebrate The Brilliant Sight Of My Devotee.

Come Slowly or Quickly, but Surely Come To Me.

Touch My Heart, and I Will Widen You To God-Knows-Where.

THE DAWN HORSE TESTAMENT OF THE RUCHIRA AVATAR

Y ou are Blessed to be alive at the time of the Greatest of Revelations—the All-Completing Revelation of Real God promised by all the religious and Spiritual traditions of mankind. The Divine World-Teacher, Ruchira Avatar Adi Da Samraj, is that All-Completing Revelation. He is the Perfect Fulfillment of that universal promise.

Ruchira Avatar Adi Da Samraj Offers you a devotional relationship which literally brings His tangible Divine Blessing into your life. For the sake of all who are moved to go beyond all the dead-ends of ordinary life and all the dead-ends of Spiritual seeking, Ruchira Avatar Adi Da

Samraj has Revealed and Given the unique Way of Adidam—the only complete Way to Realize the True and Spiritual Divine Person, Who Is Reality Itself, or Truth Itself, or Real God.

You have before you now the greatest of life-choices: How are you going to respond to the Most Perfect Revelation of Real God?

How To Respond

The Divine World-Teacher, Ruchira Avatar Adi Da Samraj, Calls you to formally become His devotee—which means to formally take up practice of the Way of Adidam, the Divinely Enlightening Way of life He has Revealed and Given for the sake of all beings.

Because those who approach Him have different heart-needs and different life-circumstances to account for, Ruchira Avatar Adi Da has created four congregations of formal approach to Him. These four congregations, together, make up the Eleutherian Pan-Communion of Adidam (or, simply, the Adidam Pan-Communion). Which of the four congregations of the Adidam Pan-Communion you should apply to for membership depends on the strength of your impulse to respond to Avatar Adi Da's Revelation and on your life-circumstance.

Take Up the Total Practice
of the Way of Adidam

(The First and Second Congregations of the Adidam Pan-Communion)

The first and second congregations of the Adidam Pan-Communion are for practitioners of the total practice of the Way of Adidam (and for student-novices, who are formally approaching the total practice of the Way of Adidam). In particular, the first congregation is for those who have dedicated their lives one-pointedly to Realizing Real God—it is the congregation made up of the two formal renunciate orders of Adidam: the Ruchira Sannyasin Order of the Tantric Renunciates of Adidam, and the Avabhasin Lay Renunciate Order of the Tantric Renunciates of Adidam. The second congregation is made up of student-novices, student-beginners, and members of the Lay Congregationist Order of Adidam (which is the general lay practicing and serving order of Ruchira Avatar Adi Da's lay devotees who have advanced beyond the student-beginner stage).

To take up the total practice of the Way of Adidam is to take full advantage of the opportunity Offered by Ruchira Avatar Adi Da Samraj—it is to enter fully into the Process of Real-God-Realization. That Process of Real-God-Realization is a unique ordeal, which necessarily requires application to a wide range of functional, practical, relational, and cultural self-disciplines Revealed and Given by Ruchira Avatar Adi Da Samraj for the sake of that Divine Process. These disciplines allow the body-mind to be made ever more available to Ruchira Avatar Adi Da's Blessing Transmission. They range from foundation practices relative to diet, health, sexuality, and work, to the core devotional practices of meditation, sacramental worship, and study of Avatar Adi Da's Wisdom-Teaching. The Way of Adidam is not a "talking" school based on merely adhering

221

to a certain philosophy or upholding a certain religious point of view. Rather, the Way of Adidam is a "practicing" school, in which you participate in the Process of Real-God-Realization with every aspect of your being.

If you want to enter fully into the Process of Real-God-Realization in the Company of Ruchira Avatar Adi Da Samraj, then you should apply to become a member of the second congregation of the Adidam Pan-Communion—and if you are moved to <u>one-pointedly</u> dedicate your life to the Process of Real-God-Realization, after a period of exemplary practice in the second congregation, you may apply to practice as a formal renunciate in the first congregation. (The life of members of the first and second congregations is described and pictured on pp. 232-36.)

When you apply for membership in the second congregation of the Adidam Pan-Communion (the first step for all who want to take up the total practice of the Way of Adidam), you will be asked to prepare yourself by taking "The <u>Only</u> Truth That Sets the Heart Free", a course of formal study and "consideration" (lasting four to six weeks), in which you examine the Opportunity Offered to you by Avatar Adi Da Samraj, and learn what it means to embrace the total practice of the Way of Adidam as a second-congregation devotee of Ruchira Avatar Adi Da. (To register for this preparatory course, please contact the regional or territorial center nearest to you [see p. 239], or e-mail us at: correspondence@adidam.org.) After completing this period of study, you may formally enter the second congregation by becoming a student-novice.

Entering any of the four congregations of Adidam involves taking a formal vow of devotion and service to Avatar Adi Da Samraj. This vow is a profound—and, indeed, eternal—commitment. You take this vow (for whichever congregation you are entering) when you are certain that your great and true heart-impulse is to be devoted, forever, to Avatar Adi Da Samraj as your Divine Heart-Master. If you recognize Avatar Adi Da as the Living

Divine Person—your Perfect Guide and Help and your eternal and most intimate Heart-Companion—then you know that this vow is a priceless Gift, and you joyfully embrace the great responsibility it represents.

As a student-novice (formally approaching the total practice of the Way of Adidam), you are initiated into formal meditation and sacramental worship, you begin to adapt to a wide range of life-disciplines, and you begin to participate in the life of the cooperative community of Ruchira Avatar Adi Da's devotees. As a student-novice, you engage in an intensive period of study and "consideration" of the Way of Adidam in all of its details. And, as your practice matures, you are given more and more access to the cultural life of the formally acknowledged practitioners of the total practice of Adidam. After a minimum of three to six months of practice as a student-novice, you may apply for formal acknowledgement as a fully practicing member of the second congregation.

If you find that you are steadily and profoundly moved to dedicate your life one-pointedly to Ruchira Avatar Adi Da Samraj and the Process of Real-God-Realization in His Spiritual Company, then, after a demonstration period of exemplary practice as a member of the second congregation, you may apply to practice as a formal renunciate in the first congregation of the Adidam Pan-Communion.

The two formal renunciate orders in the Way of Adidam are the Lay Renunciate Order and the Ruchira Sannyasin Order. The senior of the two orders is the Ruchira Sannyasin Order, which is the senior cultural authority within the gathering of all four congregations of Avatar Adi Da's devotees. The members of the Ruchira Sannyasin Order are the most exemplary formal renunciate practitioners practicing in the ultimate (sixth and seventh) stages of life in the Way of Adidam. The core of the Ruchira Sannyasin Order, and its senior governing members, will, in the future, be those devotees who have Realized Divine Enlightenment. Ruchira Avatar Adi Da Samraj Himself is

the Founding Member of the Ruchira Sannyasin Order, and will, throughout His Lifetime, remain its Senior Member in every respect.

The Ruchira Sannyasin Order is a retreat Order, whose members are legal renunciates. They are supported and protected in their unique Spiritual role by the Lay Renunciate Order, which is a cultural service Order that serves an inspirational and aligning role for all devotees of Avatar Adi Da.

First-congregation devotees have a special role to play in the Way of Adidam. Adi Da Samraj must have unique human Instrumentality—Spiritually Awakened and Divinely Self-Realized devotees—through whom He can continue to do His Divine Transmission Work after His physical Lifetime. No human being, not even one of Avatar Adi Da's Divinely Enlightened devotees, can "succeed" Ruchira Avatar Adi Da Samraj, in the way that, traditionally, a senior devotee often succeeds his or her Spiritual Master.* Avatar Adi Da Samraj is the Complete Incarnation of the Divine Person—He is truly the <u>Completion</u> of all Spiritual lineages in all times and places. Thus, He remains forever the Divine Awakener and Liberator of all beings. His Spiritually Awakened renunciate devotees will <u>collectively</u> function as His Spiritual Instruments, allowing His Blessing-Power to Pervade and Influence the world.

To become a fully practicing devotee of Avatar Adi Da Samraj (in the second congregation, and potentially moving on to the first congregation), call or write one of our regional centers (see p. 239) and sign up for our preliminary course, "The <u>Only</u> Truth That Sets the Heart Free".

---

*Adi Da Samraj has Said that, after His physical (human) Lifetime, there should always be one (and only one) "Murti-Guru" as a Living Link between Him and His devotees. Each successive "Murti-Guru" is to be selected from among those members of the Ruchira Sannyasin Order who have been formally acknowledged as Divinely Enlightened devotees of Adi Da. "Murti-Gurus" do not function as the independent Guru of practitioners of the Way of Adidam. Rather, they are simply Representations of Adi Da's bodily (human) Form, and a means to Commune with Him.

The Adidam Youth Fellowship

Young people (25 and under) are also offered a special form of relationship to Avatar Adi Da—the Adidam Youth Fellowship. The Adidam Youth Fellowship has two membership bodies—friends and practicing members. A friend of the Adidam Youth Fellowship is simply invited into a culture of other young people who want to learn more about Avatar Adi Da Samraj and His Happiness-Realizing Way of Adidam. A formally practicing member of the Adidam Youth Fellowship acknowledges that he or she has found his or her True Heart-Friend and Master in the Person of Avatar Adi Da Samraj, and wishes to enter into a direct, self-surrendering Spiritual relationship with Him as the Means to True Happiness. Practicing members of the Youth Fellowship embrace a series of disciplines that are similar to (but simpler than) the practices engaged by adult members of the second congregation of Adidam. Both friends and members are invited to special retreat events from time to time, where they can associate with other young devotees of Avatar Adi Da.

To become a member of the Adidam Youth Fellowship, or to learn more about this form of relationship to Avatar Adi Da, call or write:

Vision of Mulund Institute (VMI)
10336 Loch Lomond Road, Suite 146
Middletown, CA 95461
PHONE: (707) 928-6932
FAX: (707) 928-5619
E-MAIL: vmi@adidam.org

Become an Advocate of the Way of Adidam

(In the Fourth Congregation
of the Adidam Pan-Communion)

The fourth congregation of the Adidam Pan-Communion is for those who are attracted to the life of devotional intimacy with Avatar Adi Da Samraj and are moved to serve His world-Blessing Work, but who are not presently moved or able to take up the full range of disciplines required of members of the first and second congregations. Thus, if you embrace the fourth-congregation practice, you receive Avatar Adi Da's Spiritual Blessings in your life by assuming the most basic level of responsibility as His devotee. The fourth-congregation practice allows you to develop and deepen true devotional intimacy with Avatar Adi Da, but, because it does not involve the full range of disciplines, it always remains a beginning form of the practice of Adidam. If, as a member of the fourth congregation, you are eventually moved to advance beyond the beginning, you are always invited to transition to the second congregation and embrace the total—and, potentially, Divinely Enlightening—practice of the Way of Adidam.

A principal organization within the fourth congregation is the Transnational Society of Advocates of the Adidam Revelation. Advocates are individuals who recognize Ruchira Avatar Adi Da Samraj as a Source of Wisdom and Blessing in their own lives and for the world, and who want to make a practical response. Advocates serve Ruchira Avatar Adi Da's world-Blessing Work by actively serving the dissemination of His Wisdom-Teaching and by actively advocating Him and the Way of Adidam.

When you become an advocate, you make a formal vow of devotion and service to Ruchira Avatar Adi Da Samraj. As described on pp. 222-23, this vow is a profound and eternal commitment to Avatar Adi Da as Your Divine Heart-Master. By taking this vow, you are committing yourself to perform a specific consistent service to Avatar Adi Da and His Blessing Work, and to embrace the fundamental devotional practice that Avatar Adi Da Gives to all His devotees. This is the practice of Ruchira Avatara Bhakti Yoga—devotion to Ruchira Avatar Adi Da Samraj as your Divine Heart-Master. Advocates do the simplest form of this great practice, which Ruchira Avatar Adi Da summarizes as "Invoke Me, Feel Me, Breathe Me, Serve Me".

The advocate vow is also a commitment to make a monthly donation to help support the publication of Avatar Adi Da's supremely precious Wisdom-Literature (as well as publications about Him and the Way of Adidam), as well as paying an annual membership fee that supports the services of the Society of Advocates.

In addition, Advocates offer their services in the form of whatever practical or professional skills they can bring to creatively serve Ruchira Avatar Adi Da and the Way of Adidam.

To become a member of the Transnational Society of Advocates of the Adidam Revelation, call or write one of our regional centers (see p. 239), or e-mail us at:

correspondence@adidam.org

In addition to members of the Transnational Society of Advocates, those who live in traditional cultures around the world are invited to practice as members of the fourth congregation. The opportunity to practice in the fourth congregation is also extended to all those who, because of physical or other functional limitations, are unable to take up the total practice of the Way of Adidam as required in the first and second congregations.

To become a member of the fourth congregation of Adidam, call or write one of our regional centers (see p. 239), or e-mail us at: correspondence@adidam.org.

Serve the Divine World-Teacher
and His World-Blessing Work
via Patronage or Unique Influence

*(The Third Congregation
of the Adidam Pan-Communion)*

We live at a time when the destiny of mankind and of even the planet itself hangs desperately in the balance. The Divine World-Teacher, Ruchira Avatar Adi Da Samraj, has Manifested at this precarious moment in history in order to Reveal the Way of true Liberation from the disease of egoity. It is only <u>That</u> Gift of true Liberation that can reverse the disastrous trends of our time.

It is the sacred responsibility of those who respond to Ruchira Avatar Adi Da to provide the means for His Divine Work to achieve truly great effect in the world. He must be given the practical means to Bless all beings and to Work with His devotees and others responding to Him in all parts of the world, in whatever manner He is spontaneously moved to do so. He must be able to move freely from one part of the world to another. He must be able to establish Hermitages in various parts of the world, where He can Do His silent Work of Blessing, and where He can also Work with His devotees and others who can be of significant help in furthering His Work by receiving them into His physical Company. Ruchira Avatar Adi Da must also be able to gather around Him His most exemplary formal renunciate devotees—and such formal renunciates must be given practical support so that they can be entirely and one-pointedly devoted to serving Ruchira Avatar Adi Da and to living the life of perpetual Spiritual retreat in His physical Company. And the mere fact that Real God is Present in the world must become as widely known as possible, both through the publication and dissemination of books by and about Ruchira Avatar Adi Da and through public advocacy by people of influence.

If you are a man or woman of unique wealth or unique influence in the world, we invite you to serve Ruchira Avatar Adi Da's world-Blessing Work by becoming His patron. Truly, patronage of the Divine World-Teacher, Ruchira Avatar Adi Da Samraj, exceeds all other possible forms of philanthropy. You are literally helping to change the destiny of countless people by helping to support Ruchira Avatar Adi Da in His world-Blessing Work. You make it possible for Ruchira Avatar Adi Da's Divine Influence to reach people who might otherwise never come to know of Him. You make it possible for Him to make fullest use of His own physical Lifetime—the unique bodily Lifetime of Real God, Perfectly Incarnate. To make the choice to serve Avatar Adi Da via your patronage or unique influence is to allow your own life and destiny, and the life and destiny of all of mankind, to be transformed in the most Graceful way possible.

As a member of the third congregation, your relationship to Ruchira Avatar Adi Da is founded on a vow of Ruchira Avatara Bhakti Yoga—a vow of devotion, through which you commit yourself to serve His Work. In the course of your service to Ruchira Avatar Adi Da (and in daily life altogether), you live your vow of devotion by invoking Him, feeling Him, breathing Him, and serving Him (without being expected to engage the full range of disciplines practiced in the first two congregations). At all times, this practice is the means Ruchira Avatar Adi Da has Given for His third-congregation devotees to remain connected to His constant Blessing. In addition, Ruchira Avatar Adi Da has invited, and may continue to invite, members of the third congregation into His physical Company to receive His Divine Blessing.

If you are able to serve Avatar Adi Da Samraj in this crucial way, please contact us at:

Third Congregation Advocacy
12040 North Seigler Road
Middletown, CA 95461
phone number: (707) 928-4800
FAX: (707) 928-4618
e-mail: third_congregation@adidam.org

The Life of a Formally Practicing Devotee of Ruchira Avatar Adi Da Samraj

(in the First or Second Congregation of Adidam)

Everything you do as a devotee of Ruchira Avatar Adi Da Samraj in the first congregation or the second congregation of Adidam is an expression of your heart-response to Him as your Divine Heart-Master. The life of cultivating that response is Ruchira Avatara Bhakti Yoga—or the Real-God-Realizing practice ("Yoga") of devotion ("Bhakti") to the Ruchira Avatar, Adi Da Samraj.

The great practice of Ruchira Avatara Bhakti Yoga necessarily transforms the whole of your life. Every function, every relationship, every action is moved by the impulse of devotional heart-surrender to Adi Da Samraj.

AVATAR ADI DA SAMRAJ: In every moment you must turn the situation of your life into Ruchira Avatara Bhakti Yoga by exercising devotion to Me. There is no moment in any day wherein this is not your Calling. This is what you must do. You must make every moment into this Yoga by using the body, emotion, breath, and attention in self-surrendering devotional Contemplation of Me. All of those four principal faculties must be turned to Me. By constantly turning to Me, you "yoke" yourself to Me, and that practice of linking (or binding, or connecting) to Real God is religion. Religion, or Yoga, is the practice of moving out of the egoic (or separative, or self-contracted) disposition and state into Oneness with That Which is One, Whole, Absolute, All-Inclusive, and Beyond. [December 2, 1993]

As everyone quickly discovers, it is only possible to practice Ruchira Avatara Bhakti Yoga moment to moment when you establish a foundation of supportive self-discipline that enables you to reel in your attention, energy, and feeling from their random wandering. And so Ruchira Avatar Adi Da has Given unique and extraordinarily full Instruction on a complete range of functional, practical, relational, and cultural disciplines for His first-congregation and second-congregation devotees. These disciplines are not methods for attaining Happiness, but are the present-time expression of prior Happiness:

AVATAR ADI DA SAMRAJ: I do not require the discipline of conventional renunciation. Nor do I allow commitment to the karmas of self-indulgence. My devotees serve Me through the humorous discipline of an ordinary pleasurable life. This is the foundation of their practice of the Way of Adidam.

The "ordinary pleasurable life" of which Avatar Adi Da Samraj Speaks is not based on any kind of attempt to achieve immunity from the inevitable wounds of life. Rather, it is based on the always present disposition of True Happiness—the disposition of ego-transcendence through self-surrendering, self-forgetting Contemplation of Ruchira Avatar Adi Da in every moment. Therefore, the "ordinary pleasurable life" of Avatar Adi Da's devotees involves many practices that support and develop the simplicity and clarity of Happiness and self-transcendence. These practices are "ordinary" in the sense that they are not Enlightenment in and of themselves, but they are, rather, the grounds for a simple, mature, pleasurable, and truly human life, devoted to Real-God-Realization.

These practices in the Way of Adidam include cultural disciplines such as morning and evening meditation, devotional chanting and sacramental worship, study-"consideration" of Ruchira Avatar Adi Da's Wisdom-Teaching, formal weekly retreat days, extended weekend retreats every two to three months, an annual meditation retreat of ten days to six weeks. The life of practice also includes the adaptation to a pure and purifying diet, free from toxifying accessories (such as tobacco, alcohol, caffeine, sugar, and processed foods) and animal products (such as meat, dairy products, and eggs).

Meditation is a unique and precious event in the daily life of Avatar Adi Da Samraj's devotees. It offers the opportunity to relinquish outward, body-based attention and to be alone with Adi Da Samraj, allowing yourself to enter more and more into the sphere of His Divine Transmission.

The practice of sacramental worship, or "puja", in the Way of Adidam is the bodily active counter-part to meditation. It is a form of ecstatic worship of Avatar Adi Da Samraj, using a photographic representation of Him and involving devotional chanting and recitations from His Wisdom-Teaching.

You must deal with My Wisdom-Teaching in some form every single day, because a new form of the ego's game appears every single day. You must continually return to My Wisdom-Teaching, confront My Wisdom-Teaching.

Avatar Adi Da Samraj

The beginner in Spiritual life must prepare the body-mind by mastering the physical, vital dimension of life before he or she can be ready for truly Spiritual practice. Service is devotion in action, a form of Divine Communion.

Avatar Adi Da Samraj Offers practical disciplines to His devotees in the areas of work and money, diet, exercise, and sexuality. These disciplines are based on His own human experience and an immense process of "consideration" that He engaged face to face with His devotees for more than twenty-five years.

There is also a discipline of daily exercise which includes morning calisthenics and evening Hatha Yoga exercises. There is progressive adaptation to a regenerative discipline of sexuality and sexual energy. And, as a practical foundation for your personal life and the life of the community of practitioners, there is the requirement to maintain yourself in full employment or full-time service, in order to support the obligations of the sacred institution (the Eleutherian Pan-Communion of Adidam) and the cooperative community organization (the Ruchirasala of Adidam).

All of these functional, practical, relational, and cultural disciplines are means whereby your body-mind becomes capable of effectively conducting Ruchira Avatar Adi Da's constant Blessing-Transmission. Therefore, Ruchira Avatar Adi Da has made it clear that, in order to Realize Him with true profundity—and, in particular, to Realize Him most perfectly, to the degree of Divine Enlightenment—it is necessary to be a formally acknowledged member of either the first or the second congregation engaging the total practice of the Way of Adidam.

One of the ways in which Ruchira Avatar Adi Da Communicates His Divine Blessing-Transmission is through sacred places. During the course of His Teaching and Revelation Work, He Empowered three Sanctuaries as His Blessing-Seats. In each of these Sanctuaries—the Mountain Of Attention in northern California, Love-Ananda Mahal in Hawaii, and Adidam Samrajashram in Fiji—Ruchira Avatar Adi Da has Established Himself Spiritually in perpetuity. He has lived and Worked with devotees in all of His Sanctuaries, and has created in each one special holy sites and temples. In particular, Adidam Samrajashram—His Great Island-Hermitage and world-Blessing Seat—is Ruchira Avatar Adi Da's principal Place of Spiritual Work and Transmission, and will remain so forever after His physical Lifetime. Formally acknowledged devotees are invited to go on special retreats at all three Sanctuaries.

The Mountain Of Attention Sanctuary of Adidam

Love-Ananda Mahal

**Adidam Samrajashram
(Naitauba, Fiji)**

Ruchira Avatar Adi Da writes in *Eleutherios (The Only Truth That Sets The Heart Free)*:

I Have Come to Found (and, altogether, to Make Possible) a New (and Truly "Bright") Age of mankind, an Age That will not begin on the basis of the seeking mummery of ego-bondage, but an Age in Which mankind will apply itself, apart from all dilemma and all seeking, to the Inherently Harmonious Event of Real existence (in the Always Already present-time "Bright" Divine Reality That <u>Is</u> the One and Only Reality Itself).

In the brief period of two and a half decades, and in the midst of this "dark" and Godless era, Ruchira Avatar Adi Da has established His unique Spiritual culture. He has created the foundation for an unbroken tradition of Divine Self-Realization arising within a devotional gathering aligned to His fully Enlightened Wisdom, and always receiving and magnifying His Eternal Heart-Transmission. Nothing of the kind has ever existed before.

There are great choices to be made in life, choices that call on the greatest exercise of one's real intelligence and heart-impulse. Every one of us makes critical decisions that determine the course of the rest of our lives— and even our future beyond death.

The moment of discovering the Divine Avatar, Adi Da Samraj, is the greatest of <u>all</u> possible opportunities. It is pure Grace. How can an ordinary life truly compare to a life of living relationship and heart-intimacy with the greatest God-Man Who has ever appeared—the Divine in Person?

Call or write one of our regional centers and sign up for "The Only Truth That Sets the Heart Free", our preliminary course that prepares you to become a fully practicing devotee of Avatar Adi Da Samraj. Or sign up for any of our other classes, correspondence courses, seminars, events, or retreats. Or call to order more books and continue your reading.

Respond now. Do not miss this miraculous opportunity to enter into direct relationship with Real God.

The Eleutherian Pan-Communion of Adidam

AMERICAS
12040 North Seigler Road
Middletown, CA 95461
(800) 524-4941
(707) 928-4936

EUROPE-AFRICA
Annendaalderweg 10
6105 AT Maria Hoop
The Netherlands
31 (0)20 468 1442

PACIFIC-ASIA
12 Seibel Road
Henderson
Auckland 1008
New Zealand
64-9-838-9114

THE UNITED KINGDOM
London, England
0181-7317550

FIJI
P.O. Box 4744
Samabula, Suva, Fiji
381-466

AUSTRALIA
P.O. Box 460
Roseville, NSW 2069
Australia
61-2-9416-7951

E-MAIL: correspondence@adidam.org

We also have centers in the following places. For their phone numbers and addresses, please contact one of the centers listed above or visit our website: **http://www.adidam.org**.

Americas
San Rafael, CA
Los Angeles, CA
Seattle, WA
Denver, CO
Chicago, IL
Framingham, MA (Boston)
Potomac, MD
    (Washington, DC)
Kauai, HI
Quebec, Canada
Vancouver, Canada

Pacific-Asia
Western Australia
Melbourne, Australia

Europe-Africa
Amsterdam, The Netherlands
Berlin, Germany

The Sacred Literature of
Ruchira Avatar Adi Da Samraj

Start by reading *The Promised God-Man Is Here*, the astounding story of Avatar Adi Da's Divine Life and Work.

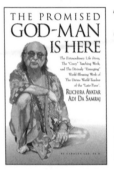

The Promised
God-Man Is Here

*The Extraordinary Life-Story,
The "Crazy" Teaching-Work, and
The Divinely "Emerging" World-Blessing
Work Of The Divine World-Teacher
Of The "Late-Time",
Ruchira Avatar Adi Da Samraj,*
by Carolyn Lee, Ph.D.—the profound, heart-rending, humorous, miraculous, wild—and true—story of the Divine Person Alive in human Form. Essential reading as background for the study of Avatar Adi Da's books.

See My Brightness
Face to Face

A Celebration of the Ruchira Avatar, Adi Da Samraj, and the First Twenty-Five Years of His Divine Revelation Work—a magnificent year-by-year pictorial celebration of Ruchira Avatar Adi Da's Divine Work with His devotees, from 1972 to 1997. Includes a wealth of selections from His Talks and Writings, numerous Stories of His

Divine Work told by His devotees, and over 100 color photographs.

$19.95, 8" x 10" quality paperback, 200 pages

THE FIVE BOOKS OF THE HEART
OF THE ADIDAM REVELATION

After reading *The Promised God-Man Is Here*, continue reading *The Five Books Of The Heart Of The Adidam Revelation*. In these five books, Avatar Adi Da Samraj has distilled the very essence of His Eternal Message to every one, in all times and places.

BOOK ONE:
Aham Da Asmi
(Beloved, I Am Da)

The "Late-Time" Avataric Revelation Of The True and Spiritual Divine Person (The egoless Personal Presence Of Reality and Truth, Which Is The Only Real God)

The most extraordinary statement ever made in human history. Avatar Adi Da Samraj fully Reveals Himself as the Living Divine Person and Proclaims His Infinite and Undying Love for all and All.

$7.95, 4"x7" paperback, 222 pages

BOOK TWO:
Ruchira Avatara Gita
(The Way Of The Divine Heart-Master)

The "Late-Time" Avataric Revelation Of The Great Secret Of The Divinely Self-Revealed Way That Most Perfectly Realizes The True and Spiritual Divine Person (The egoless Personal Presence Of Reality and Truth, Which Is The Only Real God)

Avatar Adi Da Offers to every one the ecstatic practice of devotional relationship to Him—explaining how devotion to a living human Adept-Realizer has always been the source of true religion, and distinguishing true Guru-devotion from cultism.

$7.95, 4"x7" paperback, 254 pages

BOOK THREE:

Da Love-Ananda Gita
(The Free Gift Of The Divine Love-Bliss)

The "Late-Time" Avataric Revelation Of The Great Means To Worship and To Realize The True and Spiritual Divine Person (The egoless Personal Presence Of Reality and Truth, Which Is The Only Real God)

Avatar Adi Da Reveals the secret simplicity at the heart of Adidam—relinquishing your preoccupation with yourself (and all your problems and your suffering) and, instead, Contemplating Him, the "Bright" Divine Person of Infinite Love-Bliss.

$7.95, 4"x7" paperback, 234 pages

BOOK FOUR:

Hridaya Rosary
(Four Thorns Of Heart-Instruction)

The "Late-Time" Avataric Revelation Of The Universally Tangible Divine Spiritual Body, Which Is The Supreme Agent Of The Great Means To Worship and To Realize The True and Spiritual Divine Person (The egoless Personal Presence Of Reality and Truth, Which Is The Only Real God)

The ultimate Mysteries of Spiritual life, never before revealed. In breathtakingly beautiful poetry, Avatar Adi Da Samraj sings of the "melting" of the ego in His "Rose Garden of the Heart".

$7.95, 4"x7" paperback, 358 pages

BOOK FIVE:

Eleutherios
(The Only Truth That Sets The Heart Free)

The "Late-Time" Avataric Revelation Of The "Perfect Practice" Of The Great Means To Worship and To Realize The True and Spiritual Divine Person (The egoless Personal Presence Of Reality and Truth, Which Is The Only Real God)

An address to the great human questions about God, Truth, Reality, Happiness, and Freedom. Avatar Adi Da Samraj Reveals how Absolute Divine Freedom is Realized, and makes an impassioned Call to everyone to create a world of true human freedom on Earth.

$7.95, 4"x7" paperback, 270 pages

The Seventeen Companions
Of The True Dawn Horse

O nce you have read *The Five Books Of The Heart Of The Adidam Revelation*, you are ready to continue with *The Seventeen Companions Of The True Dawn Horse*. These seventeen books are "Companions" to *The Dawn Horse Testament*, Avatar Adi Da's great summary of the Way of Adidam (p. 247). Here you will find Avatar Adi Da's Wisdom-Instruction on particular aspects of the true Spiritual Way, and His two tellings of His own Life-Story, as autobiography (*The Knee Of Listening*) and as archetypal parable (*The Mummery*). Avatar Adi Da created the Canon of His Sacred Literature in late 1997 and early 1998, and the Dawn Horse Press is currently in the process of publishing the "Seventeen Companions" and *The Dawn Horse Testament*.

BOOK ONE:

<u>Real</u> God <u>Is</u> The Indivisible Oneness Of Unbroken Light

Reality, Truth, and The "Non-Creator" God
In The True World-Religion Of Adidam

The Nature of Real God and of the cosmos. Why ultimate questions cannot be answered either by conventional religion or by science.

BOOK TWO:

The Truly Human New World-Culture Of <u>Unbroken</u> Real-God-Man

The <u>Eastern</u> Versus The <u>Western</u> Traditional Cultures
Of Mankind, and The Unique New <u>Non-Dual</u> Culture
Of The True World-Religion Of Adidam

The Eastern and Western approaches to religion, and life altogether—and how the Way of Adidam goes beyond this apparent dichotomy.

BOOK THREE:

The <u>Only</u> Complete Way To Realize The Unbroken Light Of <u>Real</u> God

An Introductory Overview Of The "Radical" Divine Way
Of The True World-Religion Of Adidam

The entire course of the Way of Adidam—the unique principles underlying Adidam, and the unique culmination of Adidam in Divine Enlightenment.

BOOK SEVENTEEN

The Basket Of Tolerance

The Perfect Guide To Perfectly <u>Unified</u> Understanding Of The One and Great Tradition Of Mankind, and Of The Divine Way Of Adidam As The Perfect <u>Completing</u> Of The One and Great Tradition Of Mankind

An all-encompassing "map" of mankind's entire history of religious seeking. A combination of a bibliography of over 5,000 items (organized to display Avatar Adi Da's grand Argument relative to the Great Tradition) with over 100 Essays by Avatar Adi Da, illuminating many specific aspects of the Great Tradition.

THE DAWN HORSE TESTAMENT

The Dawn Horse Testament Of The Ruchira Avatar

The "Testament Of Secrets" Of The Divine World-Teacher, Ruchira Avatar Adi Da Samraj

Avatar Adi Da's paramount "Source-Text" which summarizes the entire course of the Way of Adidam. Adi Da Samraj says: "In making this Testament I have been Meditating everyone, contacting everyone, dealing with psychic forces everywhere, in all time. This Testament is an always Living Conversation between Me and absolutely every one."

The Dawn Horse Press

In addition to Avatar Adi Da's 23 "Source-Texts", the Dawn Horse Press offers hundreds of other publications and items for meditation and sacred worship—courses, videotapes, audiotapes, compact discs, magazines, photos, incense, sacred art and jewelry, and more. Call today for a full catalog of products or visit our website (http://dhp.adidam.org) where you will find full-color images of all our products and on-line ordering.

For more information or a free catalog:
CALL TOLL-FREE 1-800-524-4941
(Outside North America call 707-928-4936)

Visit us on-line at **http://dhp.adidam.org**

Or e-mail: **dhp@adidam.org**

Or write:

THE DAWN HORSE PRESS
12040 North Seigler Road
Middletown, CA 95461 USA

We accept Visa, MasterCard, personal checks, and money orders. In the USA, please add $4.00 (shipping and handling) for the first book and $1.00 for each additional book. California residents add 7.25% sales tax. Outside the USA, please add $7.00 (shipping and handling) for the first book and $3.00 for each additional book. Checks and money orders should be made payable to the Dawn Horse Press.

An Invitation to Support Adidam

Avatar Adi Da Samraj's sole Purpose is to act as a Source of continuous Divine Grace for everyone, everywhere. In that spirit, He is a Free Renunciate and He owns nothing. Those who have made gestures in support of Avatar Adi Da's Work have found that their generosity is returned in many Blessings that are full of His healing, transforming, and Liberating Grace—and those Blessings flow not only directly to them as the beneficiaries of His Work, but to many others, even all others. At the same time, all tangible gifts of support help secure and nurture Avatar Adi Da's Work in necessary and practical ways, again similarly benefiting the entire world. Because all this is so, supporting His Work is the most auspicious form of financial giving, and we happily extend to you an invitation to serve Adidam through your financial support.

You may make a financial contribution in support of the Work of Adi Da Samraj at any time. You may also, if you choose, request that your contribution be used for one or more specific purposes.

If you are moved to help support and develop Adidam Samrajashram (Naitauba), Avatar Adi Da's Great Island-Hermitage and World-Blessing Seat in Fiji, and the circumstance provided there and elsewhere for Avatar Adi Da and the other members of the Ruchira Sannyasin Order, the senior renunciate order of Adidam, you may do so by making your contribution to The Love-Ananda Samrajya, the Australian charitable trust which has central responsibility for these Sacred Treasures of Adidam.

To do this: (1) if you do not pay taxes in the United States, make your check payable directly to "The Love-Ananda Samrajya Pty Ltd" (which serves as the trustee of the Foundation) and mail it to The Love-Ananda Samrajya at P.O. Box 4744, Samabula, Suva, Fiji; and (2) if you do pay taxes in the United States and you would like your contribution to be tax-deductible under U.S. laws, make your check payable to "The

Eleutherian Pan-Communion of Adidam", indicate on your check or accompanying letter that you would like your contribution used for the work of The Love-Ananda Samrajya, and mail your check to the Advocacy Department of Adidam at 12040 North Seigler Road, Middletown, California 95461, USA.

If you are moved to help support and provide for one of the other purposes of Adidam, such as publishing the sacred Literature of Avatar Adi Da, or supporting either of the other two Sanctuaries He has Empowered, or maintaining the Sacred Archives that preserve His recorded Talks and Writings, or publishing audio and video recordings of Avatar Adi Da, you may do so by making your contribution directly to The Eleutherian Pan-Communion of Adidam, specifying the particular purposes you wish to benefit, and mailing your check to the Advocacy Department of Adidam at the above address.

If you would like more information about these and other gifting options, or if you would like assistance in describing or making a contribution, please write to the Advocacy Department of Adidam at the above address or contact the Adidam Legal Department by telephone at (707) 928-4612 or by FAX at (707) 928-4062.

Planned Giving

We also invite you to consider making a planned gift in support of the Work of Avatar Adi Da Samraj. Many have found that through planned giving they can make a far more significant gesture of support than they would otherwise be able to make. Many have also found that by making a planned gift they are able to realize substantial tax advantages.

There are numerous ways to make a planned gift, including making a gift in your Will, or in your life insurance, or in a charitable trust.

If you would like to make a gift in your Will in support of the work of The Love-Ananda Samrajya: (1) if you do not pay taxes in the United States, simply include in your Will the statement, "I give to The Love-Ananda Samrajya Pty Ltd, as trustee of The Love-Ananda Samrajya, an Australian charitable trust, P.O. Box 4744, Samabula, Suva, Fiji, _____" [inserting in the blank the amount or description of your contribution]; and (2) if you do pay taxes in the United States and you would like your contribution to be free of estate taxes and to also reduce any estate taxes payable on the remainder of your estate, simply include in your Will the statement, "I give to The Eleutherian Pan-Communion of Adidam, a California non-profit corporation, 12040 North Seigler Road, Middletown, California 95461, USA, _____" [inserting in the blank the amount or description of your contribution].

To make a gift in your life insurance, simply name as the beneficiary (or one of the beneficiaries) of your life insurance policy the organization of your choice (The Love-Ananda Samrajya or The Eleutherian Pan-Communion of Adidam), according to the foregoing descriptions and addresses. If you are a United States taxpayer, you may receive significant tax benefits if you make a contribution to The Eleutherian Pan-Communion of Adidam through your life insurance.

We also invite you to consider establishing or participating in a charitable trust for the benefit of Adidam. If you are a United States taxpayer, you may find that such a trust will provide you with immediate tax savings and assured income for life, while at the same time enabling you to provide for your family, for your other heirs, and for the Work of Avatar Adi Da as well.

The Advocacy and Legal Departments of Adidam will be happy to provide you with further information about these and other planned gifting options, and happy to provide you or your attorney with assistance in describing or making a planned gift in support of the Work of Avatar Adi Da.

Further Notes to the Reader

An Invitation to Responsibility

Adidam, the Way of the Heart that Avatar Adi Da has Revealed, is an invitation to everyone to assume real responsibility for his or her life. As Avatar Adi Da has Said in *The Dawn Horse Testament Of The Ruchira Avatar*, "If any one Is Interested In The Realization Of The Heart, Let him or her First Submit (Formally, and By Heart) To Me, and (Thereby) Commence The Ordeal Of self-Observation, self-Understanding, and self-Transcendence." Therefore, participation in the Way of Adidam requires a real struggle with oneself, and not at all a struggle with Avatar Adi Da, or with others.

All who study the Way of Adidam or take up its practice should remember that they are responding to a Call to become responsible for themselves. They should understand that they, not Avatar Adi Da or others, are responsible for any decision they may make or action they may take in the course of their lives of study or practice. This has always been true, and it is true whatever the individual's involvement in the Way of Adidam, be it as one who studies Avatar Adi Da's Wisdom-Teaching or as a formally acknowledged member of Adidam.

Honoring and Protecting the Sacred Word through Perpetual Copyright

Since ancient times, practitioners of true religion and Spirituality have valued, above all, time spent in the Company of the Sat-Guru (or one who has, to any degree, Realized Real God, Truth, or Reality, and who, thus, Serves the awakening process in others). Such practitioners understand that the Sat-Guru literally Transmits his or her (Realized) State to every one (and every thing) with whom (or with which) he or she comes in contact. Through this Transmission, objects, environments, and rightly prepared individuals with which the Sat-Guru has contact can become Empowered, or Imbued with the Sat-Guru's Transforming Power. It is by this process of Empowerment that things and beings are made truly and literally sacred, and things so sanctified thereafter function as a Source of the Sat-Guru's Blessing for all who understand how to make right and sacred use of them.

Sat-Gurus of any degree of Realization and all that they Empower are, therefore, truly Sacred Treasures, for they help draw the practitioner more quickly into the process of Realization. Cultures of true Wisdom have always understood that such Sacred Treasures are precious (and fragile) Gifts to humanity, and that they should be honored, protected, and reserved for right sacred use. Indeed, the word "sacred" means "set apart", and, thus, protected, from the secular world. Avatar Adi Da has Conformed His body-mind Most Perfectly to the Divine Self, and He is, thus, the most Potent Source of Blessing-Transmission of Real God, or Truth Itself, or Reality Itself. He has for many years Empowered (or made sacred) special places and things, and these now Serve as His Divine Agents, or as literal expressions and extensions of His Blessing-Transmission. Among these Empowered Sacred Treasures is His Wisdom-Teaching, which is Full of His Transforming Power. This Blessed and Blessing Wisdom-Teaching has Mantric Force, or the literal Power to Serve Real-God-Realization in those who are Graced to receive it.

Therefore, Avatar Adi Da's Wisdom-Teaching must be perpetually honored and protected, "set apart" from all possible interference and wrong use. The fellowship of devotees of Avatar Adi Da is committed to the perpetual preservation and right honoring of the sacred Wisdom-Teaching of the Way of Adidam. But it is also true that, in order to fully accomplish this, we must find support in the world-society in which we live and in its laws. Thus, we call for a world-society and for laws that acknowledge the Sacred, and that permanently protect It from insensitive, secular interference and wrong use of any kind. We call for, among other things, a system of law that acknowledges that the Wisdom-Teaching of the Way of Adidam, in all Its forms, is, because of Its sacred nature, protected by perpetual copyright.

We invite others who respect the Sacred to join with us in this call and in working toward its realization. And, even in the meantime, we claim that all copyrights to the Wisdom-Teaching of Avatar Adi Da and the other sacred Literature and recordings of the Way of Adidam are of perpetual duration.

We make this claim on behalf of The Love-Ananda Samrajya Pty Ltd, which, acting as trustee of The Love-Ananda Samrajya, is the holder of all such copyrights.

Avatar Adi Da and the Sacred Treasures of Adidam

True Spiritual Masters have Realized Real God (to one degree or another), and, therefore, they bring great Blessing and introduce Divine Possibility to the world. Such Adept-Realizers Accomplish universal Blessing Work that benefits everything and everyone. They also Work very specifically and intentionally with individuals who approach them as their devotees, and with those places where they reside and to which they Direct their specific Regard for the sake of perpetual Spiritual Empowerment. This was understood in traditional Spiritual cultures, and, therefore, those cultures found ways to honor Adept-Realizers by providing circumstances for them where they were free to do their Spiritual Work without obstruction or interference.

Those who value Avatar Adi Da's Realization and Service have always endeavored to appropriately honor Him in this traditional way by providing a circumstance where He is completely Free to do His Divine Work. Since 1983, He has resided principally on the island of Naitauba, Fiji, also known as Adidam Samrajashram. This island has been set aside by Avatar Adi Da's devotees worldwide as a Place for Him to do His universal Blessing Work for the sake of everyone, as well as His specific Work with those who pilgrimage to Adidam Samrajashram to receive the special Blessing of coming into His physical Company.

Avatar Adi Da is a legal renunciate. He owns nothing and He has no secular or religious institutional function. He Functions only in Freedom. He, and the other members of the Ruchira Sannyasin Order, the senior renunciate order of Adidam, are provided for by The Love-Ananda Samrajya, which also provides for Adidam Samrajashram altogether and ensures the permanent integrity of Avatar Adi Da's Wisdom-Teaching, both in its archival and in its published forms. The Love-Ananda Samrajya, which functions only in Fiji, exists exclusively to provide for these Sacred Treasures of Adidam.

Outside Fiji, the institution which has developed in response to Avatar Adi Da's Wisdom-Teaching and universal Blessing is known as "The Eleutherian Pan-Communion of Adidam". This formal organization is active worldwide in making Avatar Adi Da's Wisdom-Teaching available to all, in offering guidance to all who are moved to respond to His Offering, and in providing for the other Sacred Treasures of Adidam, including the Mountain Of Attention Sanctuary (in California) and Love-Ananda Mahal (in Hawaii). In addition to the central corporate entity known as The Eleutherian Pan-Communion of Adidam, which is based in California, there are numerous regional entities which serve congregations of Avatar Adi Da's devotees in various places throughout the world.

Practitioners of Adidam worldwide have also established numerous community organizations, through which they provide for many of their common and cooperative community needs, including those relating to housing, food, businesses, medical care, schools, and death and dying. By attending to these and all other ordinary human concerns and affairs via self-transcending cooperation and mutual effort, Avatar Adi Da's devotees constantly free their energy and attention, both personally and collectively, for practice of the Way of Adidam and for service to Avatar Adi Da Samraj, to Adidam Samrajashram, to the other Sacred Treasures of Adidam, and to The Eleutherian Pan-Communion of Adidam.

All of the organizations that have evolved in response to Avatar Adi Da Samraj and His Offering are legally separate from one another, and each has its own purpose and function. Avatar Adi Da neither directs, nor bears responsibility for, the activities of these organizations. Again, He Functions only in Freedom. These organizations represent the collective intention of practitioners of Adidam worldwide not only to provide for the Sacred Treasures of Adidam, but also to make Avatar Adi Da's Offering of the Way of Adidam universally available to all.

INDEX

NOTE TO THE READER: Page numbers in **boldface** type refer to the Scriptural Text of *Eleutherios*. All other page numbers refer to the introductions, endnotes, and the back matter.

I do not simply recommend or turn men and women to Truth. I <u>Am</u> Truth. I Draw men and women to My Self. I <u>Am</u> the Present Real God, Desiring, Loving, and Drawing up My devotees. I have Come to Be Present with My devotees, to Reveal to them the True Nature of life in Real God, which is Love, and of mind in Real God, which is Faith. I Stand always Present in the Place and Form of Real God. I accept the qualities of all who turn to Me, dissolving those qualities in Real God, so that <u>Only</u> God becomes the Condition, Destiny, Intelligence, and Work of My devotees. I look for My devotees to acknowledge Me and turn to Me in appropriate ways, surrendering to Me perfectly, depending on Me, full of Me always, with only a face of love.

I am waiting for you. I have been waiting for you eternally.

Where are you?

AVATAR ADI DA SAMRAJ
1 9 7 1